Interiors Beyond Architecture

Interiors Beyond Architecture proposes an expanded impact for interior design that transcends the inside of buildings, analyzing significant interiors that engage space outside of the disciplinary boundaries of architecture. It presents contemporary case studies from a historically nuanced and theoretically informed perspective, presenting a series of often-radical propositions about the nature of the interior itself. Internationally renowned contributors from the UK, US and New Zealand present ten typologically specific chapters including: Interiors Formed with Nature, Adaptively Reused Structures, Mobile Interiors, Inhabitable art, Interiors for Display and On Display, Film Sets, Infrastructural Interiors, Interiors for Extreme Environments, Interior Landscapes, and Exterior Interiors.

Deborah Schneiderman is Professor of Interior Design in the School of Art and Design at Pratt Institute in Brooklyn, New York. She is principal and founder of deSc: architecture/design/research, a research practice focused on the emerging fabricated interior environment and its materiality.

Amy Campos is Associate Professor of Interior Design at California College of the Arts in San Francisco. She is principal and founder of ACA—Amy Campos Architect, a practice focused on durability and design with special interest in the impermanent, migratory potentials of the interior.

D1561130

Deborah Schneiderman
Amy Campos

Interiors Beyond Architecture

Routledge
Taylor & Francis Group

LONDON AND NEW YORK

First published 2018
by Routledge
2 Park Square, Milton Park, Abingdon, Oxon OX14 4RN

and by Routledge
711 Third Avenue, New York, NY 10017

Routledge is an imprint of the Taylor & Francis Group, an informa business

British Library Cataloguing-in-Publication Data
A catalogue record for this book is available from the British Library

Library of Congress Cataloging-in-Publication Data
A catalog record for this book has been requested

ISBN: 978-1-138-12497-4 (hbk)
ISBN: 978-1-138-12498-1 (pbk)
ISBN: 978-1-315-64783-8 (ebk)

Typeset in Gill Sans
by Apex CoVantage, LLC
Printed in Canada

CONTENTS

FOREWORD

Lois Weinthal

EXTRACTION

To extract and analyze helps bring clarity to a greater whole by viewing the parts—whether it be soil in a core sample to understand a building's foundation, or text from a narrative that gives hint at a larger story. The space of interiors is often viewed as part of an architectural whole. If architecture can be seen as the shell that contains the interior, then each interior can be extracted and analyzed independently. We do not often think of the interior as a core sample the way we do a soil sample, but if we could extract a hypothetical core sample that extends up from the soil and through the height of a building, the sample would reveal a set of relationships that include tectonics—some thick (concrete foundation) and some thin (veneer finishes)—along with voids both small (space between joists) and large (full height of a room). This is only a sample of building forms that would be revealed and placed in equal standing to one another through this objective lens. The remainder of what exists outside of that lens would reveal a fuller picture of the interior such as program, occupancy, materials and the temporal nature of the ever-changing interior-scape. The peripheral view from the core sample is where the analysis of the physical composition ends and the theoretical complexity of the interior reveals change faster than settling soil.

The title, *Interiors Beyond Architecture,* recognizes the complexity in defining interiors as a stand-alone discipline when history has continuously tied it to related fields or as a subset of architecture. Early departures from architecture are evident in floor plans from the eighteenth century, where rooms were isolated from adjacent spaces and furniture and cabinetmakers developed an independent style through décor. Not only did the style of the time shape the interior, but the drawing techniques took a departure from conventions in order to provide a pre-digital walk-through by unfolding interior surfaces in relationship to one another (Evans, 1997). The interior styles of the time also emerged in novels where rooms were described in great detail, leaving the architectural framework behind. This is most evident in Joris-Karl Huysmans' nineteenth century novel *Á rebours* (*Against Nature*) (1884), where the main character, Jean Des Esseintes, surrounds himself in domestic interiors with artificial environments that mock nature—in one example, noting how the experience of sea-bathing can be easily replaced with salt added to a bath (Huysmans & Baldick, 1979: 36). The extracted view of the interior as a stand-alone experience is taken further in Huysmans' novel where the interior décor has an overwhelming effect on characters, as Des Esseintes reflects on his choice of room color as a means of seduction. Huysmans sets the stage with the description: "This room, where mirror echoed mirror, and every wall reflected an endless succession of pink boudoirs, had been the talk of all of his mistresses, who loved steeping their nakedness in this warm bath of rosy light and breathing in the aromatic odors given off by the camphor-wood" (Huysmans & Baldick, 1997: 25). Interior décor impressed itself on the characters and separated itself from architecture to emerge as an independent entity.

Ultimately, the interior is a costume—interchangeable from one identity to another. As an example, Huysmans' novel utilized the interior to its greatest function at that time—a space contained within an architectural shell, decorated by trades and craftsmen under the guise of various exotic themes in order to emphasize the ability to insert an artificial environment into an architectural shell. Only the interior is ever described in such great detail. The result immersed Des Esseintes into an isolated environment where interior transcends architecture. Here, architecture loses its grasp on grounding the interior, and instead, the interior is free of earlier architectural treatise where it was yet to be identified in equal standing to the design of machines, classical orders and town planning, to name a few (Kruft, 1994).[1] Compared to the static nature of architecture, the interior is nimble and chameleon-like.

These early fissures that emerged from historical examples provide a foundation to understand what separates interiors beyond architecture. To define *interiors beyond architecture* is an aggressive statement that seeks to create a fracture, and more than a hairline fracture. In order to identify the interior as a distinct entity, the historic and conventional boundaries need to be identified in order to unleash the stronghold of architecture and allow interiors to be framed within its own intrinsic qualities.

F[R]ICTIONAL BOUNDARIES

When Campos and Schneiderman ask how we define interiors beyond architecture, they confirm the notion that differences exist between the two disciplines, as a result, a discussion ensues on how to dissolve the differences. Since the path to dissolving them is first to acknowledge the differences, then embracing these as a means of establishing what makes the interior a distinct spatial entity is necessary. Physical boundaries are intriguing and cause a great deal of friction, otherwise the physical and psychological attributes surrounding the simple wall as a boundary, ranging from the curious to mundane, would be lost. An isolated view of a wall provokes tension with the duality of this side and that. After all, every architect has an allegiance to enjoy the permeable office wall from the film *Brazil* that allows a shared, or rather territory-driven desktop to slide back and forth between two offices, only adding to the hermetic nature of each room on either side of the wall (Pryce *et al.,* 1985).

The friction between interior design and architecture also exists in the academic and professional disciplines, primarily in North America. It is no coincidence that these disciplines have gone through great pains to distinguish themselves from one another. But where the difference ultimately lies is that architecture can be held responsible for load-bearing structures whereas interior design cannot. Everything else reinforces subtle differences between the disciplines.

Campos and Schneiderman identify a segment of the built environment that inherently belongs to the realm of interiors. When evocative forms emerge from the interior, such as developments in textiles, architecture claims it until the next distraction comes along, or related disciplines such as landscape architecture, which must look further afield to define its own territory. Yet, for landscape architecture, the contrast between vertical and horizontal—building and landscape—marks a clear definition between neighboring disciplines, whereas the distinction between interior and architecture results in greater ambiguity as one is embedded in the other. Architecture spans the scale of urban planning to interior detail, which is all-encompassing and implies that the field is vast. But to extract the segment that is specifically interior and to unpack it becomes much more complicated because of the distinct set of design problems that emerge specific to the interior.

As simple as a threshold may be, it has the ability to define interior and exterior. A boundary provides clarity and can vary in thickness resulting in distinct, isolated spaces, or appear as a simple line on the ground that allows movement across. Each of these design decisions is informed by cues that dictate how a boundary should perform. Performance criteria give designers a springboard for shaping built form, where the conceptual parameters inform the physical. Frameworks help organize these parameters in the form of mapping, diagrams and notations. One boundary line that marries a conceptual framework to physical form is the prime meridian, the longitudinal line denoting 0°, in addition to acting as the location of Greenwich Mean Time at the Royal Observatory in London.[2] It is one thing to construct a physical boundary but an entirely other thing to construct one that fulfills universal meaning. In this example, the conceptual diagram and accompanying world map override the physical to identify time, upon which other universal clocks gauge in synchronicity. The line can be as thin as a thread because its presence has fallen secondary to the larger role of shaping universal time and space. Visitors to the observatory can straddle the line with a foot in both the eastern and western hemispheres, bringing great pleasure knowing that the body can occupy two spaces at once, both local and universal. The pleasure is even greater than that of the sliding desktop from *Brazil*, and uses less built form to be experienced.

P[L]ACE-HOLDERS

The prime meridian line is a physical demarcation that represents a larger universal framework. The line itself is physical and static, yet its purpose in synchronizing time is constantly on the move as time is not static. If we return to the example of the hypothetical core sample, a parallel relationship exists. The material in the core sample is tangible evidence. Yet the movement of people, furniture, curtains, doors, changing light conditions, and other non-static forms cannot be captured in the static core sample. These movements are dynamic and less predictable, which is why they often do not make it to the set of construction documents other than representations as static placeholders. When the interior is placed within the context of architectural language it fails on a long-term basis to reveal what it does best—represent the fleeting and nimble character of actions that take place on the interior.

The peripheral view outside of the core sample is where this performance criteria can be found, but is evident through the temporary activities on the interior. These actions are informed by programming needs that exist as a conceptual framework until they manifest as physical outcomes. The program allows for movement and change over time; real time, in the case of the interior, and not the amount of time it takes a building to weather. It is so quick that it is best represented through film rather than construction documents. And this is where we find interiors beyond architecture. The lens that reveals the intrinsic qualities of the interior are not bound to the same language as architecture.

The emergence of the interior as a stand-alone discipline siphoned off a number of design issues from architecture to become the expert in topics embedded in the interior, much like landscape architects have their area of expertise. Identifying the intrinsic qualities of the interior helps distinguish the discipline under its own set of qualities. In the process of extracting these issues from architecture to interior I would like to suggest that the conceptual framework of time aligns better with the interior. In order to understand time within the context of interiors, the conventional definitions need to be realigned and viewed from the lens of interior—from inside-out, versus the patriarchal view of outside-in.

TIME

The interior reveals a set of complex relationships when viewed through the lens of time and duration, and with it the activities that take place. Georges Perec's philosophical writings on the everyday place emphasis on domestic activities in *Species of Spaces and Other Pieces*. He explores the actions associated with daily routines to arrive at an inherent sense of dwelling, resulting in renaming rooms by function and senses rather than static nouns, thereby implying movement and action. This verb–noun dichotomy supports the argument for interiors as a time-based discipline. His analysis uses an apartment building, where he concludes that architects design the architectural framework and sequence of rooms that act as placeholders until getting populated with room names. Towards the end of this observation he concludes "a room is a fairly malleable space" (Perec, 2008: 28). The distinction between the room as placeholder and malleability hints at the intrinsic nature of interiors to alter and respond to the needs of dwellers. Perec continues this line of thought by developing a lens to view the model of a family as they move through daily routines of washing, eating, dressing, relaxing, and sleeping, accompanied by the corresponding room names during a timeline spanning 15 waking hours. The minimum time lapse used in the model is five minutes, suggesting the speed at which interiors change (Perec, 2008: 28–30). What emerges from his analysis are the dynamic qualities of the interior that present a truthful representation of function rather than static room names. Time is the essential factor in this model that defines the interior and allows for malleability.

MOVING FORWARD

The language of the interior excels when represented in diagrams. It allows for activities to be diagrammed, not just in two-dimensional relationships but as time-based activity. Returning to the title of this book, *Interiors Beyond Architecture*, I would argue that interiors excel beyond architecture at multiple rates of speed. The essays in this volume represent these rates of speed, whether at the speed of mobile interiors, film, or seasonal changes as seen in window displays. Because of these ranges, time and duration are necessary to reveal the intrinsic qualities of the interior. These conceptual forces shape the physical realm and open a new threshold for interiors as the go-to discipline for areas that place emphasis on occupation rather than static form.

If interiors excel beyond architecture then it is certainly a greater challenge to work with information that is fleeting, and at times unpredictable, and prompts the discipline to rewrite its theory and practice so that it leaves behind the established conventions in order for a new treatise to emerge. Campos and Schneiderman open this threshold so that the collection of authors in this volume can bring forward the attributes that transcend the conventions.

NOTES

01 Hanno-Walter Kruft's anthology *A History of Architectural Theory: From Vitruvius to the Present* provides an overview of architectural treatise such as those by Vitruvius, Alberti and Palladio. Kruft identifies the major topics covered in these historical treatise.
02 See the Royal Observatory Greenwich website on the meridian line for further information about its place in defining longitude and Greenwich Mean Time.

INTRODUCTION

Amy Campos &
Deborah Schneiderman

With *Interiors Beyond Architecture* we seek to highlight the importance of the expanding discipline of interior design today, recentering the practice within multiple alternate contexts in order to shift our essential understanding of interior design's potential. Until recently interior design has been considered either a subset of architecture or a practice of decoration and personal taste, both of which assume a physical location within the inside of a building. In this limited context the interior is often left misunderstood, making the placement of the interior within a discrete theoretical framework difficult (Kleinman *et al.*, 2011: 9).

The aim of this volume is to attempt to capture recent developments in interior design beyond architecture. There is very little authorship specifically addressing the potential of interior design applied beyond the traditional boundaries of architecture, yet interior designers are increasingly asked to practice within new and untraditional territories. We seek to establish the field of interior design not merely as a subset of architecture limited to the inverse of a building, but as a distinct practice that specifically focuses on the specialty of the *inside* as a literal and theoretical territory. It has been noted that "the dominance of architectural theory has arguably inhibited the development of critically informed interior studies" (Winton, 2013: 49). Inspired by this notion, we have sought to develop a critique of the interior that surpasses the limits of traditional architecture. Each chapter will frame the context of an identified territory and define significant interiors that engage space beyond the disciplinary boundaries of architecture, whether they exist without a building or transcend the architecture that they are within.

"Section I: Interiors without architecture" forms the basis for establishing this research and was the book's original title. The title is a play on the 1964–1965 exhibition and accompanying book *Architecture Without Architects* at the Museum of Modern Art in New York City, which celebrated cross-cultural vernacular architecture, often considered inferior to buildings designed by architects (Rudofsky, 1964). Similarly, interior design is typically considered a sub- or secondary discipline to architecture. This volume proposes an expanded examination of interior design as a practice often distinct from buildings and hence architecture. This section in particular investigates the design of interior spaces that are not within buildings but are found, for example, in subterranean earthforms, prefabricated storage containers and mobile vehicles.

Figure 0.1
Pigeon Valley between Uchisar and Göreme, Cappadocia. Photo: Alison B. Snyder

Figure 0.2
Uchisar cave hotel, interior view, Cappadocia. Photo: Alison B. Snyder

Arguably the design of the interior predates that of architecture, when we consider the very earliest human inhabitations found within naturally formed envelopes. Humans have cultivated these spaces for millennia, advancing a symbiotic relationship with natural processes in service of their own protection, climatic comfort and cultural enrichment. As noted in the chapter "Interiors formed with nature," co-authored by the editors of this volume, throughout human history we see varying tactics to cultivate the natural world towards our own benefit. The caves at Leang Timpuseng cave in Sulawesi, Indonesia contain some of the earliest records of human inhabitation, marking astrological, animal and human narratives through an accumulation of many drawings on the walls dating back almost 40,000 years (Aubert, 2014). The formation of interior space within or below the Earth's surface also has a long and rich history in human occupation. Some of these interiors have been formed almost entirely by nature, while others have been carefully carved into complex living environments. The cliff dwellings in Mesa Verde were built into a naturally formed enclosure in the cliff face, producing a village within the cliff—an interior within an interior. In Cappadocia, Turkey, volcanic cave formations naturally eroded by wind and water were then further articulated by humans as early as 1800 B.C. into a complex system of tunnels and chambers to form inhabitable interiors. In northern China's Loess plateau, yaodongs, or "house caves," were carved below the Earth's surface. In their carving the ground becomes the roof while deep courtyards cut into the surface provide entry, light, and air (Rudofsky, 1965: 15–24).

Interior design within repurposed structures that were not necessarily intended for inhabitation requires the designing of an additional interior climatic shell. The notion that an interior can be formed within an object that was not initially meant for inhabitation is precisely described by Graeme Brooker in his chapter

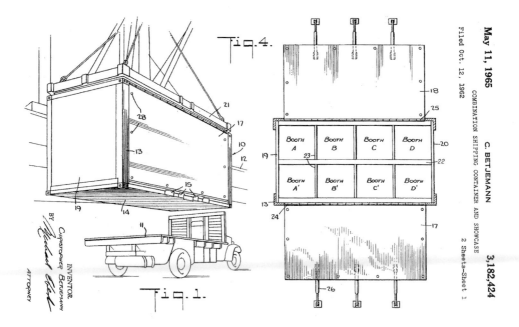

Figure 0.3

Combination shipping container and showcase US Patent 3,182,424, sheet 1 of 2. Source: United States Patent and Trademark Office, www.uspto.gov

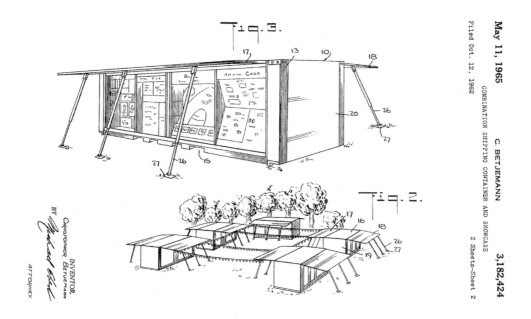

Figure 0.4

Combination shipping container and showcase US Patent 3,182,424, sheet 2 of 2. Source: United States Patent and Trademark Office, www.uspto.gov

"(Re)fit for (re)purpose." In it he explores interior space made beyond the confines of the architectured envelope (a site that is a building). The chapter articulates that the refitting of an object not intended for inhabitation demands innovation and, arguably, also disconnects a dependence of the interior on the architectured environment within which it is contained. Hence Brooker proposes a radical inversion of the previously assumed hierarchy of architects and interior designers. While the late twentieth century and early twenty-first century have witnessed a surge of proposals for container houses, it is not, in fact, a new idea. An early example of a modified, inhabitable shipping container is found in the US Patent "Combination shipping container and showcase" publication number US 3,182,424, filed on October 12 1962 by Christopher Betjemann. While the siting of interior spaces within the non-architectured envelope (a site that is not a building) is of critical importance to this investigation, arguably the formation of an interior room in a building within a non-architectured interior space is of equal relevance.

Figure 0.5
Morton Loft, interior view of petrol tank sleeping lofts, LOT-EK. Photo: Paul Warchol

LOT-EK's 2000 Morton Loft is the archetypal interior room formed from a prefabricated element. It is created from a petrol tank that is cut in half and retrofitted to form private spaces within the otherwise open loft. One half is suspended horizontally above the living space to form two sleeping lofts, and the other half is placed vertically to form two bathrooms. By working with a predefined formal element, LOT-EK had to contend with a rethinking of habitation within this non-traditional form. The relationships between the spaces inside the tank and those adjacent are completely redefined because of the lack of an "architectured" envelope. When an interior is no longer constrained by the confines of the architectured environment it can be considered freed from the ruleset affiliated with a typical architecture site (Young, 2000).

The design for mobile interiors, like those of a train, car, or boat, introduces a critical challenge to incorporate all necessary functions of the design within extreme spatial constraints. Design for these types of spaces requires adept knowledge of the human condition in order to contend with issues of privacy and publicness as well as climatic, speed, and safety requirements. In Amy Campos' chapter, "Mobile interiors," the projects cited challenge us to question ideas of territory, permanence, ownership, and scale in our daily lives. In the mid-nineteenth century the Pullman Company was formed and the future of transportation design changed forever. George Pullman, after enduring the discomfort of overnight travel by rail, recognized a market for and created a line of luxury sleeping rail cars. The designs for these overnight rail cars included a host of comforts never before imagined as a part of the travel experience. With accommodations designed and styled as opulent parlor lounges that could transform into comfortable, if compact, sleeping quarters, Pullman cars offered a new future of travel for leisure. The enjoyment of the journey was as important to Pullman as the destination, and thus began a continued expectation for well-designed transport integral to our notion of a modern, mobile lifestyle. We see in Campos' chapter the contemporary lineage of these foundational design strategies.

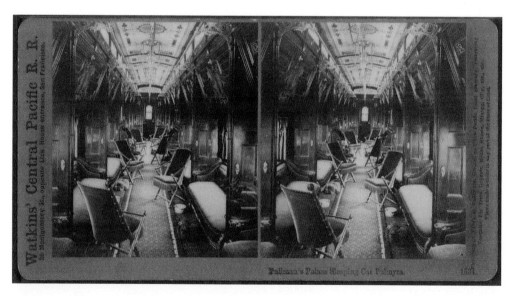

Figure 0.6
The Miriam and Ira D. Wallach Division of Art, Prints and Photographs: photography collection, the New York Public Library. *Pullman's Palace Sleeping Car Palmyra (interior)*. Retrieved from http://digitalcollections.nypl.org/items/510d47e0-b6b4-a3d9-e040-e00a18064a99

In "Section II: The autonomous inside" the authors explore a broad range of interiors that either transcend or do not acknowledge the buildings that they are housed within. Inhabitable artworks, window displays, and film sets provide purely aesthetic or sensory experiences that challenge how we occupy the world. Spatial experiences absent of traditional programmatic elements, typical code requirements, and other pragmatic limitations surprise us and change our expectations about how our environments operate.

Inhabitable art can take the form of relatively permanent installations and large-scale furniture that can house multiple persons, affecting the social behavior of those within them, as evidenced in Allan and Ellen Wexler's 2006 *Two Too Large Tables* installed in Hudson River Park in New York City. In Alex Schweder's chapter, "Artists occupying interiors occupying artists," several artworks made by artists for their own occupation are examined. He contends that such installations are interior "expressions of their inhabitants' identities, struggles, and relationships; but that they produce them as well." The works investigated by Schweder have a powerful precedent in Chris Burden's 1971 *Five Day Locker Piece*. Burden inhabited the interior of locker Number 5 at the University of California, Irvine, for five days without leaving. He utilized the locker directly above for the storage of a five-gallon bottle filled with water for his consumption, and the locker below contained an empty five-gallon bottle for the collection of urine. In this chapter the symbiotic relationship between space and its inhabitation, inhabitants, and environment is examined under atypical scenarios with unusually restricted scale, stability, and timelines of use.

Figure 0.7
Two Too Large Tables. © Allan and Ellen Wexler

In her chapter "Interiors for display and on display," Karin Tehve likens the shop display to the museum display and notes that museums and department stores "contain striking similarities at the point of contact with the visitor or consumer. The shop window has its parallel in the diorama, and each variant above makes liberal use of vitrines, platforms and similar case work."

Figure 0.8
Le Bon Marché à Paris (1875), an early modern department store. Photo: Albert Chevojon

The notion that interior space is seasonal and consumable significantly distinguishes interior design from architecture. In their volume *Architectures of Display: Department Stores and Modern Retail*, Lasc, Lara-Betancourt, and Petty propose that department store displays, introduced in the mid-nineteenth century, challenge traditional hierarchies and replace typical materials of architecture—"brick and mortar, paint and stone"—with those of the decorated interior—"theatrical props, tantalizing fabrics, lighting, wax mannequins and artificial flowers"—to create what they term "a real architecture of display."

Film sets are autonomous environments, narrating their own context. They remind us of the fantastical or historical role that the space we inhabit (or that inhabits our imagination) can play in the construction of our shared cultural experience. In her chapter "Framing interiority: film sets and the discipline of interior design," Alexa Griffith Winton analyzes the sets of several films and determines that in each of them "critical elements of the practice of interior design—independent of architecture—are used to create and support the narrative, the atmosphere and the depiction of characters." She also notes that "the films prioritize the interior and the critical ways in which characters inhabit and respond to it; architecture is depicted only schematically as a way of providing context, and otherwise bearing little relationship to the physical and symbolic elements that comprise the interiors of the films."

Infrastructural interiors operate under a completely different set of priorities than traditional interiors, often simultaneously accommodating more conventional programs as well as more complex and unique systems. As Deborah Schneiderman's "Infrastructural interior" chapter defines, such interiors might exist within a structure that is not a building, within a building that was not constructed originally for human inhabitation, or as a networked interior that exists across buildings rather than as an isolated interior. Places of infrastructure, which can be defined as physical places of interconnectivity, a utility that provides the infrastructure for a public service, or as a replicable building model, are critical sites for interior investigation. When one considers infrastructure, the typical association is with physical places of interconnectivity for transportation, communication, utilities, and other basic services. In a more current definition, infrastructure has become understood far beyond this limited scope to include replicable building models that maintain an organization or information network.

"Section III: The hyper-interior" coincides well with the title of this volume, *Interiors Beyond Architecture*. The *Oxford English Dictionary* defines hyper, from the Greek *huper*, as meaning "over, beyond." "The hyper-interior" investigates interiors that are extreme, of another discipline, and not interior in the traditional sense at all. The designing of interiors beyond architecture provides opportunities to test strategies in extreme conditions that can later be applied to more typical scenarios. In his chapter "Interiors for extreme environments," Gregory Marinic notes that film set designs are among several devices that "framed design discourse within the realm of hermetically enclosed spaces." For example, Stanley Kubrick's 1968 film *2001: A Space Odyssey* was "primarily envisioned as interior spaces of spaceships and domed cities of a future world." He then contends that the interior of Destiny, NASA's permanent orbit research station from 2001, appears, purposefully or not, as a real-life manifestation of the interiors depicted in *2001: A Space Odyssey*.

If we describe interior design expertise as the artful curation of the human experience in space, then many recent design experiments in the occupation of extreme spaces that are well outside traditional architectural settings offer new ground for the application of interior ideas. Extreme environments are often engineered for efficiency and safety, without much attention paid to supporting and sustaining human well-being (Davies, 2016: 145). The interiors of NASA's 1973 Skylab by Raymond F. Lowery have been described as similar to Buckminster Fuller's Wichita Dwelling Machine of the mid-1940s (Kleinman and Adams, 2012: 225). Buckminster Fuller's Dwelling Machine was inspired by optimistic visions of an ecologically efficient, endlessly

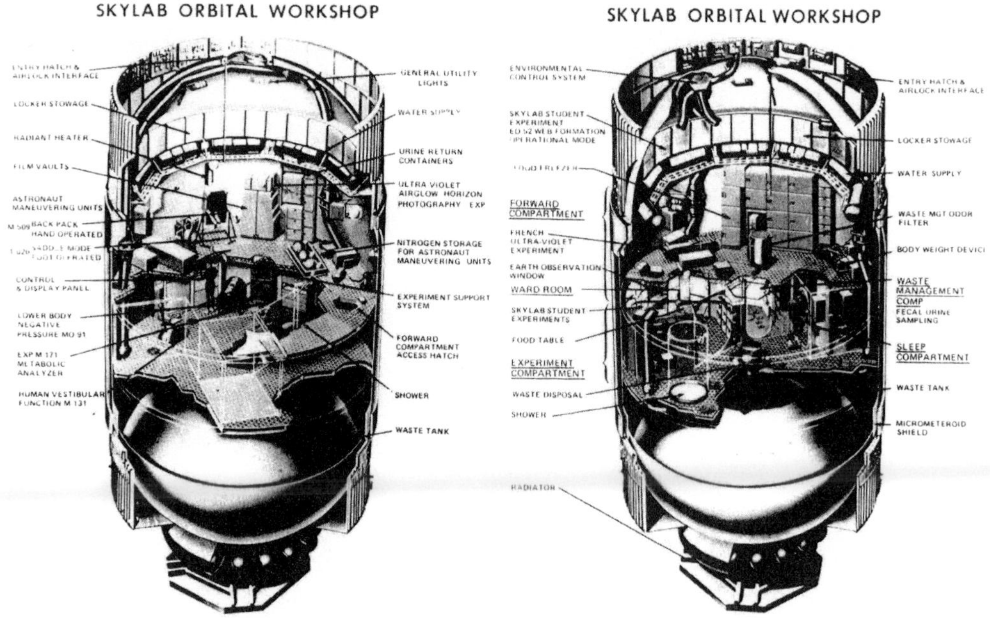

SKYLAB ORBITAL WORKSHOP

SKYLAB ORBITAL WORKSHOP

Figure 0.9
Skylab orbital workshop diagram. Image: NASA

ORBITAL WORKSHOP
WARDROOM TABLE

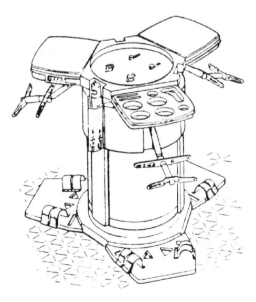

Figure 0.10
Skylab orbital workshop table diagram. Image: NASA

Figure 0.11
Interior of a prison, Giovanni Battista Piranesi, 1743

customizable future for living. The Wichita house was designed with an open plan for living, with all utilities housed in a central core and occupants meant to define their own lifestyle within the Dwelling Machine. This was radically different from the housing of the day, with highly articulated rooms for each particular activity (eating, sleeping, cooking, and socializing). In the design for Skylab, everyday social factors, including hierarchical delineation, are also omitted; the dining table in NASA's Skylab module was designed to be triangular so that when three crew members were eating together no one would be at the head of the table (Twyford, 2016: 159).

Some spatial strategies approach the interior as if it is a natural landscape: a continuous ecological system made up of layers of atmospheres and processes all integrally linked through a shared environment. In his chapter "Interior landscapes," Brett Snyder contends that "interior landscape challenges the conventional interior—its non-porous surfaces, regular ground, and hidden ecologies." He states that "interior landscape is not simply the conscious integration of materials normally found in landscape, but instead it is applying methodologies typically associated with landscape architecture to the inside." As a historical reference to this contemporary exploration he cites the eighteenth-century work of Giovanni Battista Piranesi. Snyder describes Piranesi's drawings as "inflected by natural systems; light, atmosphere, fragmented geometries, and the connection to uncontrollable environments just beyond reach."

This integral relationship between natural phenomena and inhabitation is carefully questioned in a pair of landscape installations from the late 1970s. Walter De Maria's referential pieces, *The Vertical Earth Kilometer* (1977) in Kassel, Germany, and *The Broken Kilometer* (1979) in New York City, offer a way to consider relationships between the vastness of the landscape and experiential qualities of inhabitation. *The Vertical Earth Kilometer*, installed where two paths intersect at the site of the recurring Documenta Art Fair, is a kilometer-long brass rod inserted vertically into the earth, leaving only the five-centimeter end exposed and flush with the surface a visitor walks on. Its counterpart, *The Broken Kilometer*, is a series of 500 brass rods whose total cumulative length also equals one kilometer. These rods are permanently installed in a gallery in Soho in a grid 45 feet wide by 125 feet deep, with each rod spaced an additional five millimeters apart from the previous rod front to back, such that the first row is 80 millimeters apart while the last is 570 millimeters apart. These sibling pieces ask viewers to consider immense scale and vastness through the unseen depth of *The Vertical Earth Kilometer*, piercing six geological layers that took 79 days to drill through, countered by the rather insignificant visual presence of the five-centimeter exposed end. Scale is confronted alternately in *The Broken Kilometer* via the intangible, imagined weight of the visually striking repetition of the polished rods, illusively glinting and reflecting the gallery as viewers move around the installation. De Maria's pair of works asks us to consider a simultaneous inhabitation of the immensity of the landscape imagined only through the reference of the body; in one case through the minute proportion of the end of the rod and in the other case through the forced perspectival repetition of the rods as one moves past the rods receding into the space. The layers of the Earth and the dimensions of a gallery in a dense urban fabric are equally referenced as landscapes critical in our perception of ourselves in space.

The design of exterior space can be likened to the condition of the interior when that exterior space takes on qualities of privacy, inhabitation, and enclosure (physical or alluded to). Exterior spaces with interior conditions are evidenced on the very intimate scale of a courtyard or backyard or in the very public realm of a piazza, square, or even city street. In their chapter "Exterior interiors: the urban living room and beyond," Joanna Merwood-Salisbury and Vanessa Coxhead argue that the contemporary global city is as much an interior condition as an exterior one. The courtyard of the sixteenth century Uffizi Palace in Florence is an early and fitting example of an exterior space with an interior condition. Surrounded by walls, the courtyard is inhabited as a defined public interior space (Rowe, 1978). Walled pocket parks, such as Paley Park (1967)

Figure 0.12
Walter De Maria, *The Vertical Earth Kilometer*, 1977. © The estate of Walter De Maria. Photo: Nic Tenwiggenhorn

Figure 0.13
Walter De Maria, *The Broken Kilometer*, 1979. © The estate of Walter De Maria. Photo: Jon Abbott

in New York City, can be considered an archetypal example of exterior interior, surrounded on three sides by buildings, with movable seating encouraging passers-by to stop a moment and engage with the environment. The Tactical Urbanism movement described by Merwood-Salisbury and Coxhead facilitates the appropriation of exterior spaces as small as parking spaces or as large as Times Square in New York City.

This volume offers optimistic and ambitious terrain for the discipline of interior design. Covering the design of interior spaces from the vantage point of human occupancy, we hope that this book acts as a provocation towards an expanded interior design discipline.

SECTION I

INTERIORS WITHOUT ARCHITECTURE

Inspired by the 1964–1965 Museum of Modern Art exhibition and catalog *Architecture Without Architects*, this section proposes a vastly expanded conception of interior and lays the groundwork for a renewed under-standing of the discipline that reaches beyond the walls of traditional buildings. The intention of the exhibition *Architecture Without Architects* was to expand limited views of what is accepted as architecture and hence open up architectural knowledge to less established and affirmed priorities and techniques. Interiors without architecture are found among the earliest human inhabitations within naturally formed structures. Today, as resource consumption comes to the forefront of any designer's agenda, we see interiors produced through the appropriation of prefabricated, reused enclosures not originally intended for human occupation. Interior design expertise applied to the extremely precise spaces within moving vehicles offers a whole range of design concerns and strategies only addressed within these non-architectural environments.

PROVOCATIONS:

- How might our cultural history be reframed through an interior-focused discourse?
- Can interiors without architecture motivate a more environmentally conscious future?
- What social, aesthetic, and material opportunities emerge when an inhabitable interior is sited in an enclosure not meant for human occupation?

01 Interiors formed with nature

Amy Campos & Deborah Schneiderman

The cultivation of inhabitable spaces forms the foundation of our human culture. The very earliest human inhabitations are found in naturally formed interior spaces. Humans have shaped these spaces for millennia, advancing a symbiotic relationship with natural processes in service of their own protection, climatic comfort and cultural enrichment. The caves at Leang Timpuseng in Sulawesi, Indonesia are some of the earliest records of human inhabitation, marking astrological, animal, and human narratives through drawings on the walls dating back almost 40,000 years. The caves themselves have protected these depictions from the elements for many generations. Throughout human history we see varying strategies to manipulate the natural world towards our own benefit. In this chapter we will discuss the formation of interior spaces within natural habitats that preference the interior through subterranean excavation, additive cultivation, and subtractive material processes.

SUBTERRANEAN

The formation of interior space below the surface of the Earth by means of subtraction, or troglodytism, has a long and rich history in human occupation. Some of these interiors have been formed almost entirely by nature, while others have been carefully carved into complex living environments. The caves within the volcanic formations of Göreme in Turkey were naturally eroded by wind and water, then further articulated by humans to form a complex system of inhabitable tunnels and chambers. Occupation of these caves, which are still lived in today, dates from as early as 1800 B.C. (*National Geographic*, n.d.). Similarly in Sicily's Anapo Valley, chambers were carved into the hillside nearly 3,000 years ago. The chambers were originally constructed as a burial site, but in the Middle Ages were converted into multi-storey dwellings connected by an infrastructure of interior corridors. In northern China's Loess plateau, yaodong, or subterranean dwellings, were carved below the Earth's surface. In the carving of the yaodong the ground becomes the roof, while deep courtyards cut into the surface provide entry, light, and air. The land performs simultaneously as landscape and inhabitation, with planted fields as roofs above, and, below, enclosures for residents and civic structures, supported by carved earthen arches (Rudofsky, 1964: 19–23). The underground siting naturally creates thermal mass which maintains a temperate interior.

The subterranean Villa Vals from 2009 is sited directly downhill from Zumthor's 1996 Therme in Vals, a Swiss Alpine village at an elevation of 4,100 feet. The primary impetus for the underground siting of Villa Vals, designed by SeARCH and Christian Müller Architects (CMA), was arguably its close proximity to the world-renowned Therme Vals. The design team was determined not to compete with the

Figure 1.1
Uchisar cave hotel, interior view, Cappadocia. Photo: Alison B. Snyder

architecture nor block the views of Therme Vals while also maintaining the perception of an untouched landscape. Light and air are provided to the villa through an architecturally prominent embedded façade that also constructs a protected patio in the form of an inverted spherical opening. Often described as a hole, the patio delivers light to and views from the villa's interior. While the façade, fabricated from Valser quartzite recovered from the site, is visually prominent from the foot of the hill, it is hidden when viewed from the Therme Vals above. Like the subtractive inhabitations that have been carved into hillsides for thousands of years, Villa Vals benefits from the natural thermal insulation that being underground provides. In addition to being thermally insulated, the villa incorporates a ground-source heat pump, radiant floors, heat exchanger and uses only hydroelectric power generated by the nearby reservoir (Zeigler, 2011: 213).

Villa Vals is composed of two structures; in addition to the subterranean structure, an existing two-storey barn was incorporated into the plan and forms the entrance to the villa. The barn is sited downhill from the primary inhabitation; visitors enter the property through it and proceed along a 72-feet-long subterranean corridor, compressed in darkness, and are finally released into the villa at the light-filled patio. The corridor terminates in a fork, with entrances to the kitchen on the left and the patio on the right. The form of the 1,700 square-feet interior is enclosed within a simple concrete box that incorporates a retaining wall measuring 52 feet wide, 26 feet deep and two and half storeys high, with one concave face forming the inverted spherically open patio and façade (Broome, 2010: 56–58). The envelope of the inhabitable interior is confined to a generic box, which does not take advantage of the possibility for a subterranean interior to wander in a

Figure 1.2
Villa Vals, exterior view. Photo: Iwan Baan

more labyrinthine manner, as with some of cave interiors found in Sicily, Italy, and Cappadocia in Turkey. However, while the plan is bound rectangularly, sectionally the spaces within the simple envelope are more loosely articulated to heighten spatial experience. The rooms are irregularly stacked so that each can gain access to light, air, and views from the spherical hole while also providing inhabitable space proportioned to enhance function and occupation. Hence the Villa Vals section is aligned with a Loosian Raumplan, with floor elevations at varying heights determined to maximize light and views. The interior section is notable in that it clearly depicts architecture as furniture. Rather than bed frames being placed on top of floors, creating under-utilized voids beneath them, floors lift to become raised platforms that allow for higher ceilings and more expansive views in the living spaces below. The interior becomes an articulated architectonic to support a more considered living environment. While the plan of the house remains relatively contained as a simple underground rectangular void, the section is configured as a well-considered interior, designed carefully to address inhabitation and experience within each of the spaces. Villa Vals, sited below the Earth's surface and within nature, is protected and insulated. Because it does not visually interfere with its surroundings and omits no legible architectural presence, it is released from requirements to adhere to a vernacular style.

Figure 1.3
Villa Vals, interior view demonstrating shifted section. Photo: Iwan Baan

ADDITIVE

The method of forming interior space by sculpting nature has a well-founded precedent in the construction of topiary (hedge) mazes. Dating to as early as the thirteenth century, topiaries formed a labyrinthine interior that was not within a building but rather bounded by nature. The topiary maze, while formed from nature, is arguably a planned and constructed environment, since the topiaries were not an existing natural condition but rather were planted with the intent to build the maze and purposefully pruned to construct the resulting manicured interior.

R&Sie(n)'s 2007 Spidernethewood, sited in France near Nimes, appropriates the strategy of manipulated nature as labyrinth as its primary space-making tactic. In the design of Spidernethewood, the architects R&Sie(n) employ a polypropylene mesh textile, installed well beyond the boundary of a more typical archi-tectonic structure, to restrain vegetation and form an imprecise interior space bounded by nature. From the exterior the residence is imperceptible. Within this exterior formed by the vegetated mesh, a more typically built structure is experienced as an inner interior. A similar strategy can be found in the design of Mies van der Rohe's 1951 Farnsworth House, in Plano, Illinois. The trees that surround the clearing and envelop the house can be regarded as the true exterior and protective façade of the residence. The structure can then be

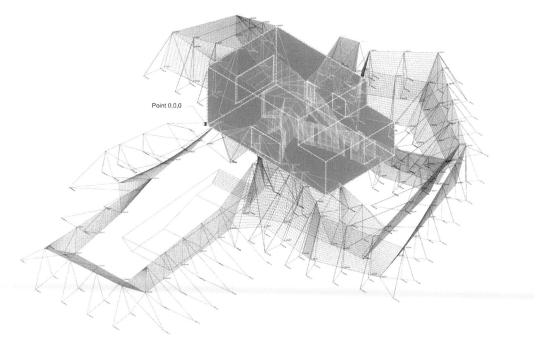

Point 0,0,0

Figure 1.4
Axonometric drawing. Spidernethewood, new-territories/R&Sie(n) 2007. F Roche

Figure 1.5
View of netted passage at construction completion. Spidernethewood, new-territories/R&Sie(n) 2007. F Roche

considered as an inner interior within a naturally formed exterior envelope. In both cases the exteriors are more temporal and change over time—qualities more often attributed to the interior—while the interiors are defined by more fixed conditions, a clear inversion of our traditional expectation for the relationship between interiors and architecture (Schneiderman, 2016: 95).

The façade of Spidernethewood will become more wooded as existing and newly planted vegetation develops, and it will also change seasonally. The project's interior is articulated as one with a series of inhabitable layers. The outer envelope is formed at the moment of restraint where mesh and vegetation intersect

Figure 1.6
View of netted passage, one year after construction completion. Spidernethewood, new-territories/R&Sie(n) 2007. F Roche

and encompasses a series of paths, a 450 square-meter concrete structure, a swimming pool and a secondary layer of textile (Di Raimo, 2014: 33–36). The outermost of the three interior layers occurs within the space between the mesh and the concrete structure; the middle interior layer, or the interior within the interior, is enclosed by the concrete structure.

Though not formed by nature, Adam Kalkin's 2001 Bunny Lane House, in Bernardsville, New Jersey, transforms a former exterior space into an interior that surrounds a more traditional structure. Rather than using vegetation, Kalkin constructed a prefabricated Butler Building steel exterior envelope over an existing house (Bergdoll and Christensen, 2008: 176–177). The new envelope transformed the exterior of the original house from façade to interior partition and converted the former yard into interior living space. Similarly, the exterior envelope of Spidernethewood, in this case vegetation restrained by mesh, bounds the concrete box that begins as exterior space and transforms it over time into an inhabitable interior environment. The mesh at

Figure 1.7
View toward inner interior, one year after construction completion. Spidernethewood, new-territories/R&Sie(n) 2007. F Roche

once creates a formed boundary between landscape and the concrete box as well as facilitates the growth of the vegetation to naturally transform these into interiors and blur the definition between exterior and interior.

Materiality enhances the project's interiority. Concrete, the structure's interior material, is repeated in the swimming pool, while the meshed textile exterior envelope is continuous with a more tightly woven textile inner layer. This denser textile layer passes through the concrete structure, creating an extended threshold and blurring the boundaries to form the innermost interior layer (Hensel and Turko, 2015: 212–213). This layering of spaces significantly transforms what was one exterior space into an inhabitable interior environment. The labyrinthine passages within the meshed spaces further test the boundaries between interior and exterior as they transform into more tightly woven textile tunnels that form the innermost layer of the interior within the concrete structure. Through this complex transformation and overlapping of textile—a materiality typically relegated only to the indoors—inhabitants are constantly passing through boundaries and layered thresholds that question exterior/interior space within an interior formed from nature.

Figure 1.8
Exterior view, one year after construction completion. Spidernethewood, new-territories/R&Sie(n) 2007. F Roche

SUBTRACTIVE

We do not often see entire buildings built with the singular objective of creating interior space and form, omitting a preoccupation for exterior façade and architectural image. The Bruder Klaus Field Chapel by Peter Zumthor from 2007 (Pallister, 2015) and The Truffle by Ensamble Studio from 2010 offer a unique contemporary case for interiors formed with subtractive natural processes. In both cases the construction processes are manipulations of natural forces including earth, fire, cultivated plant material, and animal inhabitation.

Figure 1.9
Field Chapel interior, 2007. Photo: Till Niermann

Zumthor's Field Chapel is a simple structure with no artificial environmental controls—electricity, plumbing, heating, or ventilation. The homage to the agriculturalist patron saint of Switzerland was constructed by selecting and trimming 120 of the straightest pine trunks from a local forest and arranging them into a precise teardrop-shaped mass to produce the formwork for 24 layers of concrete cast around the trunks. Once these cast layers had set around the mass the trunks were set alight and burnt out of the concrete structure, leaving a void with a drop-shaped oculus at the top. The residue of the pine trunks produces a smoke-blackened, fluted interior enclosure, in stark contrast to the clean, rectilinear quality of the exterior. The *process* of construction here is essential to the legibility of interior inhabitable qualities of space—the smell of char, the blackness of the soot, the residual inverted fluting that the pine trunks form. This procedure, of constructing a mass that is later subtracted to reveal an inhabitable interior, is also seen in Ensamble Studio's project playfully titled The Truffle.

The Truffle encloses an interior void within an interior form created through multiple, multi-specied inhabitations on a single site over the course of a year (García-Abril, 2010). It is located in Costa da Morte on the Atlantic coast of Spain and is as much an excavated object as it is a designed formula for a series of natural processes and ongoing inhabitations. Ensamble Studio approached the project with an extended timeline, a magnificent site and a specific and limited palette of material processes, including the employment of a hungry cow named Paulina.

The conception of The Truffle could only be realized with Paulina's participation. Almost 600 years earlier, Brunelleschi's scheme for the Santa Maria del Fiore Duomo in Florence (Scaglia, 1970) included many brilliant innovations, but it was particularly ingenious in accommodating oxen's inability to walk backwards. Brunelleschi recognized that incredible efficiency and capability could be realized by capturing the strength of an ox to hoist material to the 180-feet-high base (Mueller, 2014) of the dome while also accommodating the time-consuming effort of constantly re-harnessing the ox in the opposite direction with every load up and down. By inventing a clutch-operated, multi-speed hoist that included a reversible gear system, Brunelleschi solved the problem of getting the extremely heavy building material for the dome to the starting point at the top of the nave walls. Ultimately his scheme was chosen because of his magnificent invention—the reversible ox hoist.

For The Truffle, Ensamble Studio planned for a series of subtractive excavations that would be filled and cast and excavated again to produce an inhabitable environment resembling the form of a truffle. They began by digging a large hole in the soil of the existing site and carefully used the soil excavated to create a dam wall within which to cast the house. They then almost completely filled the dammed hole with hay bales, stacked like pixels; the bales were stacked intentionally as an inverted mass of inhabitable space that would eventually emerge on the site. Hay was selected for its massive and textural properties as well as its appeal as food for Paulina. Just enough space was left between the hay and the dirt to pour concrete between the two materials and over the hay bales, completely enclosing the mass of hay within a cast concrete mold of the dirt excavation. After leaving the heavy concrete to settle and set firmly, Ensamble dug out The Truffle, much like the method for extracting the namesake delicacy from the earth. The excavation revealed an inversion of the soil dam, an interior cast as exterior face. Then, using stone-cutting equipment, Ensamble cut two ends of The Truffle off to reveal the hay mass of the inner interior cast.

Finally Paulina was introduced to the site as a young calf, employed to slowly grow and nourish herself with the hay. A year later the cow emerged from the site fully grown, having eaten her way through the entirety of the hay. An incredible, slumped cast void inside The Truffle house was left as a by-product of Paulina's inhabitation of the site. Only visible once Paulina ingested all the interior mass, the hay compressed under the weight of the concrete as it set and deformed to produce a uniquely indeterminate interior character—a fuzzy textured collection of almost, but not quite, the same scaled units legible in the interior cast.

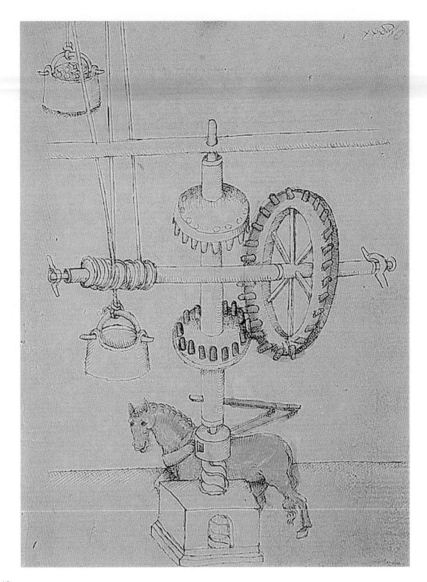

Figure 1.10
Veduta Generale della Gru di Brunelleschi, 1430. Image: Mariano di Jacopo detto Il Taccola. Collection: Biblioteca Nazionale Centrale di Firenze

The designers enclosed the two cut openings with a window and door and built in a few minimal furnishings for bathing, sitting, and sleeping—mechanisms for a post-occupancy human inhabitation. A fireplace provides warmth to heat the mass of cast concrete, and a void left by hay bales through the roof provides ventilation for the chimney.

The excavated dirt face of the structure is left almost entirely alone. Aside from the removal of dirt to access the structure, no cleaning or trimming of the structure was performed. This leaves an earthen lump without much definition, aside from a few legible layers of expanded form where the weight of the wet concrete pushed the dirt outwards—more an expression of material performance than architectural ambition.

Figure 1.11
The Truffle exterior under construction. Photo: Ensamble Studio

Figure 1.12
The Truffle with Paulina, the cow, under construction. Photo: Ensamble Studio

Figure 1.13
The Truffle interior under construction. Photo: Ensamble Studio

Figure 1.14
The Truffle interior view looking in. Photo: Roland Halbe

The layered processes of subtractive excavations, both human and animal, and casts at The Truffle suggest built form that is purely interior: an interior cast (the hay) within a cast of an interior (the dirt hole). It is a void inverted and then inverted again to form an interior in an interior. The Truffle is an interior with no exterior, produced through the careful cultivation of processes of material manipulation and multi-specied inhabitation.

Figure 1.15
The Truffle interior view looking out. Photo: Roland Halbe

CONCLUSION

Interior space formed with the express intention of cultivating and utilizing natural material and processes has existed since the beginning of human settlement. The act of transforming and inhabiting an existing environment is the definition of interior design practice. Interiors formed within natural environments, without the articulated expression of architecture, suggest new forms of material manipulation, methods of construction, and aesthetic preoccupation. The act of cultivating one's environment and the act of inhabiting it are integrally linked. With the case studies offered in this chapter we can imagine a new set of priorities in our built environment that embrace ongoing and symbiotic construction, inhabitation, and change over time.

02 (Re)fit for (re)purpose

Graeme Brooker

> While the design processes of architecture and interior design share the same procedural sequence
> and a core discipline vocabulary, interior design, both as a discipline and in its product, is (or can be)
> free of the weight of architecture.

(Hildebrandt, 2004)

'Fit for purpose' is a phrase often used to describe an entity, such as an object or an institution, that is well suited or equipped for its designated role. It is sometimes used to describe the legitimacy of forms of governance, and whether regulatory processes are appropriate and relevant in their utilization. Whichever way the expression is used, it describes a way of critiquing the utility of something and determining whether it is good enough, or useful enough, for the job it was designated to undertake.

(Re)fit for (re)purpose describes, and exemplifies, what may happen when the life and the meaning of a particular object or entity is extended through its reuse. It will examine the idea that any useable thing, such as a particular object or building, can be (re)fitted for a purpose that it was never intended to accommodate. Using three exemplars, it will propose that these processes usually involve the careful and innovative engineering of any existing objects, usually to make new interior spaces. These processes are undertaken in order to make environments and elements capable of being transformed into something they were never intended to house, or to be. A (re)fit for (re)purpose approach will transform redundant or obsolete objects, elements, spaces and buildings, as well as in-use matter, by adapting them in such a way that they become refitted and thus rehabilitated. This approach negates the usual dependence on an architectured environment, the space in which an interior is often housed. Instead this essay will explore some examples of what interior space is like when it is made beyond the realms of the architectured envelope, in what I will term a *post-architecture* environment.

POST-ARCHITECTURE

Usual practice in the construction of an interior space is a dependence on the architectured environment within which it is contained. Because of this, a close disciplinary and professional connection has endured. This relationship has not always been straightforward. Historically it has been one where the subject of the interior was often considered compliant and deferential to what is usually perceived as its older and more established built-environment partner.

In the recent past this acquiescence has evolved to become a relationship where the newer, unregulated and potentially more agile discipline of the interior has been contesting the presupposed order of this association. This is for a number of reasons. First, in a world of finite resource the repurposing of the existing, a fundamental principle and elemental process of the design of the interior, has become an increasingly significant and sustainable alternative to new-build. Second, the agility and flexibility of the role and boundaries of the interior designer, propagated by a broad, reflexive and non-regulated education, have supplied designers with the predisposition and sensibility to assume and undertake numerous roles in the work of making all kinds of objects and spaces. This position often includes assuming the tasks and the responsibilities of other built-environment specialists. Third, in the twenty-first century an increased propensity for the temporal has ensured that the agility and *time-effective* dimension of the subject have compounded its value immensely within a *time-sensitive* built-environment context. Therefore, these challenges to presupposed and traditional associations in built-environment subjects, compounded by what is often referred to as the contemporary 'post-disciplinary' environment (Bremner and Rogers, 2013, Kirkham and Weber, 2013, Buscher and Cruikshank, 2009), have ensured that the many conventions of the association between architecture and the interior are beginning to change.

Another challenge to these orthodoxies can be located in the ambiguous condition of the subject. Often considered to be a problematic condition, it is said that the interior is *unfixed*. In what is actually the subject's *raison d'être* (Brooker, 2015), the multiplicity of voices that form its history, the lack of consensus over its title and regulation, even ambiguities over where the realm of the interior begins and ends, ensure a vibrant and energetic culture of enquiry within the subject. This is perpetuated through a continual quest to explore title, scope and remit in its research, education and practice.

In short, the ambiguous condition of the interior lends the subject an agility that is propagated through the constant attempt to verify its condition and means. It is not an overstatement to say that the limitations of the habitual dependence on the architectured environment have not only been discharged, but have been superseded by the discipline's conviction in a requirement to keep reinventing itself. In the decade that has passed since the publication of Hildebrandt's essay, cited above, the interior has become not only free of the weight of architecture but is now well beyond the limitations of the envelope in which it has traditionally resided.

If this is so, what forms of interior emerge beyond, or post, architecture? By this I mean what are the outcomes when the relationships between the interior and the architectural envelope are subverted and then negated? What happens when the architectural envelope, the traditional foundational condition of the interior, is no longer fit for purpose?

READY-MADES

> An ordinary object elevated to the dignity of a work of art by the mere choice of the artist.
>
> (Girst, 2003)

In the early twentieth century, Marcel Duchamp defined the idea of the ready-made. As Breton and Eluard described it (in the statement cited earlier, and often wrongly attributed to Duchamp), they portrayed the process of constructing the ready-made as one of selecting, and therefore elevating, the everyday object or carefully chosen thing. The ready-made approach foregrounded *choice* as the primary strategy for creating art. This was partly due to an attempt by Duchamp to move away from what he described as a purely *retinal art*, one that foregrounded the visual appearance and hence aesthetic of an object or element. Instead the ready-made approach established *choosing* something already made – something already imbued with meaning, associations and connotations – as the same as the act of fabricating, painting and sculpting does in more traditional forms of art. To give new meaning to an object already in production, and all of the associations that this brings, is to enable a process of creating by inserting an object into a new context, scenario, narrative; giving it new meaning along with its existing associations.

Ready-made processes and methodologies for making and creating objects and environments have persisted throughout the twentieth and twenty-first centuries. They are still considered as primary forces of creativity. In *Postproduction,* published in 2010, Nicholas Bourriaud stated:

> It is no longer a matter of starting with [a] 'blank slate' or creating meaning on the basis of virgin
> material but of finding a means of insertion into the innumerable flows of production.
>
> (Bourriaud 2010: 17)

He went on to say that:

> Artists who insert their work into that of others contribute to the eradication of the traditional
> distinction between production and consumption, creation and copy, ready-made and original work.
> The material they manipulate is no longer primary.
>
> (Bourriaud 2010: 13)

A ready-made approach to constructing interior space erases the traditional distinction between the architectured environment and the interior: it foregrounds the selection of material that is no longer primary. Instead it favours materials that are often already used and that can be refitted and repurposed for a new use. When the interior is sited within a post-architectured environment, and it is created within another vessel or envelope, the acts of selection, choice and the subsequent editing of these conditions become critical. The act of *choosing* alters or disrupts the act of the creative process. It emphasizes the practice of *selection* as opposed to the more traditionally orientated processes of *creation*.

Duchamp described a ready-made approach to using off-the-peg materials to make something new as being either one of two categories: *assisted* or *not assisted*. The *not assisted* concerned use of the raw material; the object or element that was to be reused was uncorrected, unaided or imitated. *Unassisted* ready-mades were works that took objects like the bottle-rack, the urinal and bicycle handlebars and used them as found, without any additions or changes to their material form. Conversely, *assisted* ready-mades reused objects through adding to their material form. This was undertaken with regard to the existing meaning of the object being incorporated and adapted to the new material added to the extant. The outcome was a ready-made that could be considered, that could be construed, as a composite construct. Any added-to element has these characteristics.

In the recent past, *post-architectured* environments have adopted the shipping or cargo container as the primary ready-made object chosen to house new interior space. The surfeit of shipping containers has meant they are cheap to buy, and it is easy to adapt them and construct an environment within. Often too expensive to ship empty across the world, containers are considered to be waste once they have undertaken a journey and so are sold off cheaply. The container as a ready-made element, able to be refitted and repurposed for a variety of new uses, has become omnipresent; its reuse has become a byword for cheap, sustainable, easily attainable built space. Container reuse makes sense when they are in abundance and need is great, resources are scarce, and people require shelter, such as for disaster relief.

Their proportions, strength and rigidity predispose them to be adapted for human-scaled occupation and to the creation of off-the-peg interior space. They can be stacked and remodelled, they are cheap and in endless supply, and are ultimately sustainable as they can be cut apart wilfully and reused. They offer a sturdy, budget-conscious, prefabricated environment, one that can be readily adapted and changed to contain a wide variety of new uses. The ready-made container lends itself to (re)fitting and (re)purposing for its adaptation as an interior space. Here are three examples as to how it can be utilized.

Building with ready-mades

After the Kobe earthquake of 1995 in Japan, Shigeru Ban set up the Voluntary Architects Network (VAN), an association of architects and students at Keio University that carries out emergency projects in post-disaster situations across the world. The group's work has ranged from the temporal to the more permanent, and has often included the use of ready-mades or found solutions that can be sustainable, budget efficient and expedient in both the time taken for construction and the amount of material there is to hand. This has included a system of paper partitions used to spatially divide the large gymnasium that the survivors of the 2004 Niigata earthquake were required to inhabit; the partitions afforded the hundreds of refugees some privacy and respite from the disaster in their temporary shelter in the sports hall near the disaster site. Learning from this experience, a more improved paper partition system (PPS4) was erected for the refugees of the 2011 Tôhoku earthquake and tsunami. In this system the project had evolved to incorporate connectors that no longer needed nails, thus ensuring a quicker and easier construction, and cotton fabric screens that could withstand regular opening and closing. Ban and his team erected about 2,000 of these systems for 50 refugee facilities.

The paper log house was first tested after the Kobe earthquake and then utilized in the Philippines in the aftermath of Typhoon Haiyan (locally called Yolanda) in November 2013. Previous log houses were slow to construct but these ones needed to be erected quickly and in high volume. The frame was constructed from ready-made cardboard tubes and then clad with woven bamboo and plastic sheets. Sandbags and beer crates were used as the foundations.

In all the projects, expediency in both action and in obtaining the material with which to execute ideas is of utmost importance. As Shigeru Ban says about these projects:

> They often say I was considering the relationship between architecture and the environment early on, but it's a misunderstanding. I did not start using paper tubes or recycled paper in architecture because of the widespread rise in consciousness of environmental issues. I was simply thinking of how to put weak materials to use as they were, so that there wouldn't be any waste.
>
> (Ban, 2014: 104)

Container housing

Building with ready-made and off-the-peg materials ensures that post-disaster demand can quickly be met through the supply of everyday matter. This can also be the case when ready-made materials are at hand to be used as complete enclosures. This was the situation for the temporary housing project for Onagawa, a small fishing town in Miyagi prefecture on the east coast of Japan. Along with many other towns and villages, Onagawa was devastated by the March 2011 tsunami. The destruction meant that quick action was required to house survivors and to restore forms of civic life. The only cleared flat land available for the emergency shelters was a baseball field in the upper part of the town.

Figure 2.1
Container housing: each container was carefully craned into position. © photography Hiroyuki Hirai. Image
courtesy of Shigeru Ban Architects/VAN

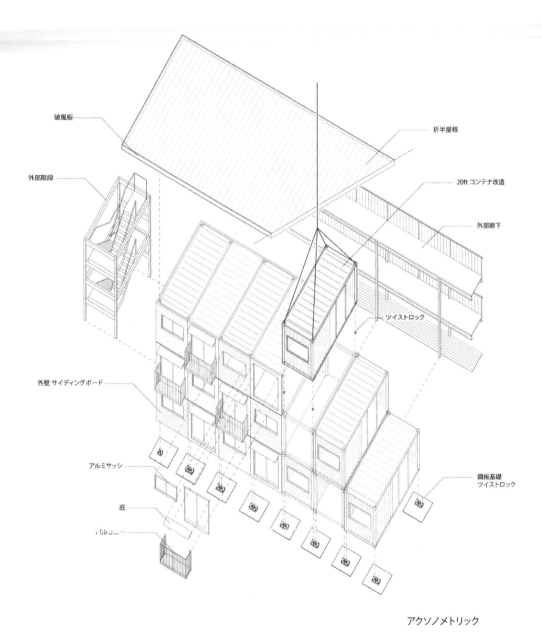

破風板

折半屋根

外部階段

20ft コンテナ改造

外部廊下

ツイストロック

外壁 サイディングボード

アルミサッシ

鋼板基礎
ツイストロック

庇

バルコニー

アクソノメトリック

Figure 2.2
Once placed into position, each container was made habitable through being modified with windows, doors, and balconies. © Image courtesy of Shigeru Ban Architects/VAN

VAN deployed a large number of disused shipping containers across the site, stacking them into two or three storeys laid out in nine residential blocks of two or three container dwellings, with stairs at either end of a block and a balcony providing resident-only access to the upper levels.

The largest blocks were for four inhabitants and utilized three containers to make a dwelling of up to 40 square-metres in size. The smallest was 20 square-metres for accommodating one or two people. A middle-sized unit was constructed using two containers and provided a temporary dwelling of 30 square-metres.

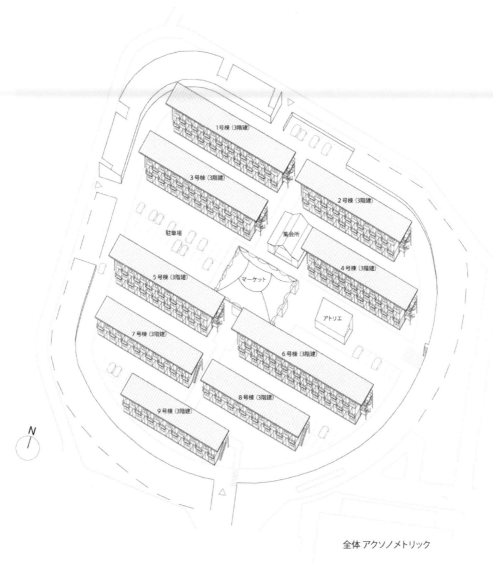

Figure 2.3
'The container houses were aligned to form a 'village' within the baseball field enclosure'. © Image courtesy of Shigeru Ban Architects/VAN

Figure 2.4
Container housing: the new development created a comfortable and secure container housing system for the traumatized residents.
© photography Hiroyuki Hirai. Image courtesy of Shigeru Ban Architects/VAN

Figure 2.5
Container housing: whilst basic, the interiors provided all of the amenities needed for its occupants.
© photography Hiroyuki Hirai. Image courtesy of Shigeru Ban Architects/VAN

A pair of containers each with a communal, open living space made up each residential block. Stacking the containers in a chequerboard pattern created variegated, open living spaces between the containers and ensured the development created a comfortable and secure container housing system.

The utilization of the shipping containers for a quick and off-the-peg solution to a disaster negated any requirements for a slower architectured solution. Instead the dimensions and qualities of the units created a post-architectured solution to provide safe and secure dwellings for the traumatized families after the tsunami.

Push-Button House

> I'm not into the container per se. It's what I can do with it emotionally: transforming a commodity into poetry, the vulgar into the sublime.
>
> (Gordon 2008: 22)

When used as a domestic environment, the anonymous and banal containers can be transformed into something quite different. The Push-Button House, designed in 2009 by Adam Kalkin, is housed inside a standard 20-feet container. It was so named because, at the push of a button, all four walls of the container can be opened or closed, revealing a domestic space inside.

Figure 2.6
Push-Button House: the interior is in stark contrast to the corrugated rusted steel shell in which it is contained. © Adam Kalkin/ Industrial Zombie www.inzombie.com. Photo: Peter Aaron/Esto

Figure 2.7
Push-Button House: the interior is revealed to show a refined space with wooden floors, sumptuous upholstery and coffee-table lamps. © Adam Kalkin/Industrial Zombie www.inzombie.com. Photo: Peter Aaron/Esto

Figure 2.8
The cosy domestic appearance is topped off with an ornate chandelier. © Adam Kalkin/Industrial Zombie www.inzombie.com. Photo: Peter Aaron/Esto

Figure 2.9
Push-Button House: heavy-duty hydraulic arms open the crate to reveal the sumptuous interior. © Adam Kalkin/Industrial Zombie
www.inzombie.com.

The walls are opened or closed by the use of heavy-duty hydraulic arms. Once opened the interior is revealed as a refined space with wooden floors, sumptuous upholstery and coffee-table lamps; all in stark contrast to the corrugated, rusted steel shell inside which it is contained.

As Kalkin says:

> All the finishes inside are milky and human and delicate… all trapped inside this heavy mechanical torso.
>
> (Gordon, 2008: 21)

The coffee tables and rugs, the mahogany benches and leather settees, along with the inviting double bed and cosy domestic appearance, are topped off with an ornate chandelier, in contrast to the brutal ready-made aesthetic of the host's exterior.

> I was looking for a kind of traditional elegance, something that screams good taste.
>
> (Gordon, 2008: 21)

The walls of the seven and a half ton house each weigh a ton and could crush the inhabitants as they are lowered, a fact that Kalkin likens to the brutality of the seemingly sweet and traditional domestic space. The vulgarity of the container and all that it stands for is transformed into a sublime domestic space.

Figure 2.10
Push-Button House: the banality of the crate is evident from the outside. © Adam Kalkin/Industrial Zombie www.inzombie.com.
Photo: Peter Aaron/Esto

Kalkin's obsession with the container has led to him constructing a variety of other homes and environments using the standardized box construction. Yet each project confounds the relationships between inside and out. The usual reliance of an interior on the architectured host is subverted by his repurposing of the container. The contrast between the traditional and cosy domestic interior and the brutal exterior is not only heightened by the reuse of the ready-made container, it is deliberately provocative in order to subjugate the domestic space. The post-architecture environment subverts the traditional relationships between inside and outside. It is made deliberately provocative by the heightening of the cosy appearance of domesticity within the container; the bespoke qualities of the interior with the off-the-peg qualities of the container.

Figure 2.11
MuMo: the museum between destinations. Image kindly supplied by Ingrid Brochard and Arno Devo © tall&ginger.com

MuMo

The Musée Mobile (MuMo) is a museum that travels to its audiences instead of them coming to see it. It is a contemporary art museum inside a shipping container that has travelled through France, Cameroon and Ivory Coast in order to show schoolchildren modern art.

The children, aged between six and 11 and in groups of 14, are invited into the museum without their teachers to spend 45 minutes exploring the works of art. They are accompanied by two child psychologists who ask the children to explore their thoughts, ideas and feelings about the art without any sense of an authoritarian figure present – but, instead, with a sense of freedom and of being listened to. Founder Ingrid Brochard secured funding from French companies such as Peugeot-Citroën and Total and commissioned 15 artists to produce work for the museum that they then loaned for the trip. Among those contributing their work were James Turrell, Ghada Amer, Muarizio Cattelan, Cheri Samba and Pierre Huyghe. Paul McCarthy contributed a giant inflatable pink rabbit that is strapped to the container's roof; it is fully inflated to make a huge sign when the museum is in position to receive the children. The museum, designed by Adam Kalkin, is housed in a large shipping container that sits on the back of a truck and, when in position, is hydraulically unfolded into four different rooms.

Each room contains artworks, paintings, videos and installations. MuMo has been visited by at least 68,000 schoolchildren, a number certain to grow over the years.

Figure 2.12
MuMo: the museum in use and full of children, with the Paul McCarthy inflatable rabbit announcing its presence. Image kindly supplied by Ingrid Brochard and Arno Devo © tall&ginger.com

looks like regular truck when travelling

deck can be used for art when museum is up.

Push Button skyscraper Museum for kids in Africa

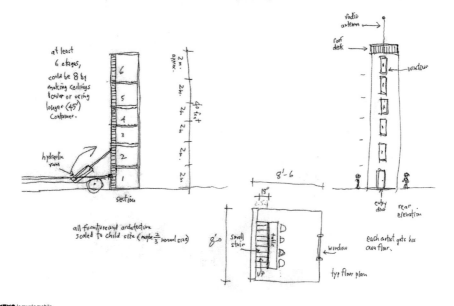

at least 6 etages, could be 8 by making ceilings lower or using longer (45') container.

hydraulic ram

section

all furniture and architecture scaled to child size (maybe 2/3 normal size)

radio antenna

roof deck

window

entry door

rear elevation

each artist gets his own floor.

8'-6

18" = 2.54

8'-0

small stair

window

UP

typ floor plan

10 **MUMO** le musée mobile

Figure 2.13
MuMo: concept sketch of how the crates can be formed to make the museum. Image kindly supplied by Ingrid Brochard and Arno Devo © tall&ginger.com

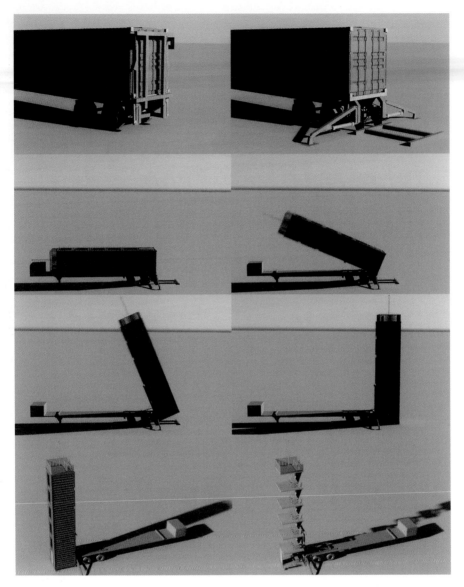

Figure 2.14
MuMo: early ideas showed the containers being off-loaded and stacked in a tower. Image kindly supplied by Ingrid Brochard and Arno Devo © tall&ginger.com

CONCLUSIONS

The standard shipping container is a simple object… what then is so revolutionary about this particular box? Put simply, it is the fact that its size, shape and form were agreed upon, made standard, and applied on a near universal basis.

(Martin 2016: 32)

Figure 2.15
MuMo: on arrival at its destination a hydraulic system of pumps opens the museum and positions the crates on the back of the truck.
Image kindly supplied by Ingrid Brochard and Arno Devo © tall&ginger.com

(Re)fit for (re)purpose suggests that exemplars of interior space that are no longer required to be located in a carefully considered architectured environment are beyond, or post, architecture. Creating interior space beyond the boundaries of any architectured environment allows designers to innovate beyond the tropes and cues that a traditional host setting may propose. The fabrication of an autonomous interior entity can foreground experimentation, and will often focus design possibilities into a search for new and unusual types of space where living, working, playing, acculturating and socializing, as well as refuge and learning, can take place. When the interior inhabits spaces that are post-architecture, the (re)fitting of environments for a new use (re)purposes specific elements and prepares them for new activities and different modes of inhabitation unfettered by the particulars of the envelope in which they reside.

The processes of refitting and repurposing extant material pose interesting questions regarding value, waste and obsoletion. When something is no longer able to accommodate the use or function it was designated for, it will often be turned into waste. In this phase of its lifecycle it is considered shorn of any value and unfit for its intended or initial purpose. As well as introducing issues around lifecycle and the discarding of unwanted matter, refitting and repurposing ensure the extended life of redundant matter. The processes transform the understanding and value of matter in a variety of ways. Tim Edensor states in *Industrial Ruins: Space Aesthetics and Materiality* that during these processes:

> The commodity, as well as other objects, appears as an entity which possesses a fixed meaning and use-value, and when these are exhausted or irrelevant, the subsequent loss of exchange value turns it into waste.

> (Edensor, 2005: 104)

The process of transforming waste into rehabilitated matter alters use-values and breathes life back into exhausted or obsolete entities. Whichever way this process is initiated and repurposing is undertaken, the refit of anything starts with the selection of matter to be adapted; the choice and edit of refitted and repurposed matter are critical. Normal practice is for the interior to be sited inside an architectured environment, one from which it might take some of its spatial tropes and cues. Often it is considered beholden to understanding the qualities of the host envelope, and then the designer can choose to defer or refer to these entities. As we have seen, when the interior no longer needs to be housed within an architectured environment it becomes free of the weight of the envelope in which it was once housed. It is conceived within a host that is regarded as an entity with no discerning qualities apart from its fundamental size; it is an entity with no substance, qualities or designed intentions and which was never intended to house an interior. Yet its refitting and repurposing, with a new and unusual use, irrevocably alters its redundant condition and fills it with new life.

03 Mobile interiors

Amy Campos

Mobile environments (land, air and water vehicles) are typically manufactured in multiples as a consumer product rather than custom-built for a pre-determined user in a specific location, and so they offer design innovations that accommodate a variety of situations and body types in order to maximize their use and desirability to consumers. Land vehicles are limited to specific spatial width and length to fit on standard roads and be able to maneuver within precise turning radii. Boats contend with buoyancy and hydrodynamic form. Air and space vehicles have a whole host of requirements that deal with aerodynamics at high speeds and variable atmospheric pressures and oxygen levels. Among many other critical design conditions, vehicles typically have a small allotment of space per person, making this category of interior habitation robust with unique precision in detail, materiality, and efficiency. Because these spaces are mobile, and house people while in motion, they must also meet specific criteria including relatively brief duration of use, durability of material under various stresses, stability, safety, and comfort of passengers. The design of mobile interiors influences the way one perceives the exterior environments beyond and impacts on how one might experience that larger environment with fellow travelers. With the development of various technologies related to travel and mobility over the last 200 years it is clear that the ability to move quickly from one place to another has become an indispensable aspect of modern life. Mobility today is an essential privilege and the spaces designed to move the world's diverse populations reinforce important cultural and social interactions with our environment and with each other.

In this chapter, three specific case studies will be discussed. First, the early 20th Century development of the "open road" ideal in North America that firmly established a shared cultural love for natural landscapes anyone with access to transport was free to enjoy. This evolved ideal today suggests novel working processes for interior design, as seen in the new Cricket trailer by Taxa Inc., reviewed in detail. Atelier Manferdini's Bianca Cruise Ferry on Lake Biwa in Japan provides an excellent design example through which to discuss the desire for a shared group leisure experience. Finally, mobility for all and issues of accessibility, efficiency, and public identity are discussed with a thorough evaluation of the New Bus for London by Thomas Heatherwick.

THE OPEN ROAD AND THE AESTHETICS OF EFFICIENCY

More than 100 years ago two simultaneous developments in the United States set the groundwork for an epic fascination with and commitment to mobility and design. The National Park System was established in 1916 (nps.gov, 2016) as an essential government entity in the country and a foundational component of the modern American identity. Around the same time, Ford Motor Company and other American car manufacturers were producing cheap, reliable cars that most middle-class Americans could afford (Slade, 2006) and the national railways were rapidly expanding the reach of their lines (Pullman-museum.org, 2016). An ability to move at greater speeds around the continent expanded many people's imagination of the world, and the national parks inspired people to explore newly accessible natural wonders. Mobility became synonymous with freedom and a tangible opportunity to pursue one's own happiness through travel and mobile leisure.

Figure 3.1
Camping at Stoneman Mountain, NPS History Collection (RL003471)

As people increasingly accessed unfamiliar environments, they required new facilities for living while on the move. Vast camping grounds popped up and cars and trains were stuffed full of equipment and gear for the many travelers' needs. Following the tradition of covered wagon trains, people began to utilize camping trailers to bring their homes with them on the road. More recently known as recreational vehicles, or RVs, they offered most of the comforts of home in a relatively compact, well-designed package. Recreational vehicles promote a comfortable, mediated connection to the landscape and ease of access to unfamiliar environments. Many RVs are designed for larger and larger footprints and now come complete with large-screen televisions, extensive climate control, and other luxuries found in a typical American home, producing an inclusive experience where the outdoors are mostly experienced as moving images seen through picture windows.

Figure 3.2
NPS History Collection. Photo: Jonathan Blair (HPC-00535)

We see in this 1964 image of an RV camp in Yellowstone National Park the domestic environment spilling into the landscape, producing interior-like outdoor experiences. The laundry lines strung between trailers define an implied room, cordoning off the outdoors and extending the interior of the trailer into the surrounding landscape. Attitudes about freedom and leisure in the outdoors evolved to be integrally tied to interior design. Eventually the comforts of home began to take over and impede one's experience of being outside.

A contemporary counterpart to the enclosed environments of modern recreational vehicles is the Cricket trailer by Taxa, Inc. While most RVs are increasingly produced as mobile domestic environments

Figure 3.3
Model Cricket trailer by Taxa Outdoors: interior view looking out of the side door. Photo courtesy of Garrett Finney, 2016

for users to be primarily inside, the Cricket is designed as a habitable environment that enables you to be outdoors. Designed in Houston, Texas, by Garrett Finney, a former senior architect for NASA's Habitability Design Center, the Cricket combines the essential qualities of a tent, a traditional camping trailer and a cargo-toting truck bed with the precision of a space shuttle. Developed beyond just the aesthetics of the house made mobile, Finney wanted to produce a more specific and careful environment for comfortable habitation in the context of the outdoors. The Cricket embraces an aesthetic of efficiency, minimal but useful technology, and accommodates customization for individual living requirements and preferences.

Finney was inspired by Buckminster Fuller's book, *Operating Manual for Spaceship Earth*, as well as his experiences working at NASA. He started to rethink the modern camping trailer by detailing a list of what he calls "performance criteria" (Finney, 2016) for each environment. In the words of Buckminster Fuller, "we start by inventorying all the important, known variables that are operative in the problem" (Buckminster Fuller, 1969.) Finney's technique was learned and modified from his time working directly with engineers to include quantitative criteria such as being lightweight and being able to hitch to another tow vehicle, as one might expect when designing a vehicle for transport. He also inventories qualitative performance criteria such as simultaneity; for example, the kitchen counter must accommodate the ability to "gut a fish, change a diaper" (Finney, 2016), or hold and charge an electronic device to "play music." What is most intriguing about this hybridized process, developed through Finney's early career, is the inclusion of very specific and extensive human-centered criteria. Finney's role at NASA and in effect his contribution to design has been "to write people into performance calculations" (Finney, 2016). He recognized early on at NASA that the relationship

Figure 3.4
Model Cricket trailer: kitchen with under-counter cubbies, 12-volt USB charging, sink with fold-down cover and universal attach points. Photo courtesy of Garrett Finney, 2016

of people and space is symbiotic, involving "millions of interacting systems" (Finney, 2016) that are calibrated through their organization and association into a functioning, habitable environment.

Designed simultaneously from the inside out and the outside in, the Cricket is a congruous solution that accommodates the performance of speed, lightness, and aerodynamics equally with the performance of the human body in space, ergonomics, and space for habitation. Intentionally, there is no disconnect between the interior and the exterior environment. Finney and his team worked in full-scale cardboard mock-ups to perfect every detail. The carefully designed interior is meant to embrace the outside as an integral part of its space and program.

The Cricket offers a stark white and aluminum interior shell, neutral woods, and grey marine fabrics countered by a few hits of bold color. Bright colors tend to designate operable components that can fold up, pull down, expand, and rotate. Much like the sequenced color-coding of aircraft flags and controls, the aesthetic of the Cricket harkens to a precision of performance within the trailer. The white interior walls are powder-coated insulated aluminum panels that reflect light and keep the space perceptibly clean and expansive in order to accommodate both spatially and visually the user's multicolored and multi-textured gear. The aluminum skeleton expresses the vehicle's engineered efficiency and provides an opportunity for built-in, nondescript perforations. Users can hang extra clothing or bungee-cord gear out of the way, or install hand-holds and supports for campers with varying physical abilities.

The Cricket can provide up to four sleeping spaces, two on benches that become a sleeping surface when the table is lowered to match the height of the bench seat and two more on mesh cots suspended from

Figure 3.5
Model Cricket trailer: view of V-berth bench/bed/storage with table lifted, suspended cot above and rear hatch with window (shown closed). Photo courtesy of Garrett Finney, 2016

Figure 3.6
Model Cricket trailer: view from V-berth towards kitchen with reflective ceiling and walls, universal attach points in ceiling and walls, cross ventilation through hard-shell and soft pop-up surfaces. Photo courtesy Garrett Finney, 2016

the ceiling. The kitchen is a simple design, often providing smart, double-duty components. The sink comes with a fold-down cover to provide more counter space when not in use. The shelves underneath the kitchen counter store food items and house the instant hot water device for the sink and shower.

When the trailer is parked, the roof of the Cricket can pop up with tent-like fabric infills to accommodate a standing head-height inside or fold down to fit easily into a typical American garage. This surface holds an optional roll-away shade structure to further blur the boundaries between interior and exterior inhabitable space. The roof also doubles as a cargo shelf with room for carting bikes, canoes, and other equipment on the outside of the trailer, or, as Finney notes in his initial design criteria, to provide space for dancing, sitting and looking.

The interior and exterior design of the Cricket facilitates an experience of the natural landscape by meeting varied and simultaneous performance criteria. It emphasizes a specific experience of the outdoors that is not coddled in a hermetic and replicated domestic environment, but rather makes the myriad experiences of living outdoors accessible to diverse users who may find camping prohibitively difficult or simply uncomfortable.

THE SHARED LEISURE EXPERIENCE

As much as early travel within the US displayed a preference for the individual's freedom to move, there has long been a fascination with shared experiences of new environments. These shared leisure experiences were accessible to those who could afford to participate, setting an implied social status through one's ability to participate in travel. Mobility here is most obviously privileged and the design of these larger vessels reflects aspirations of luxury and exclusive shared experiences of the environment.

By the 1970s the airline industry was growing rapidly, with an increasing population of flyers choosing from more and more airlines. In this competitive landscape, Braniff Airlines became a startling success, laying the framework for a business and branding collaboration model that would be repeated by countless companies in many industries for decades to come. Braniff engaged a host of designers, notably the fashion icon Emilio Pucci, the interior and object designer Alexander Girard, and the artist Alexander Calder in various collaborations to revamp the entire flying experience for customers. Harkening to the total and immersive experience of early rail travel on Pullman's luxury sleeping cars, mentioned in the introduction of this book, Braniff sought to produce a unique and immersive design experience while traveling by air. Noting the need for significant distraction and entertainment during longer flights, Braniff hired designers to rework everything from card decks and attendants' uniforms to the cutlery and dishware used in the planes and airport lounges, to the exteriors of the fleet and the interiors of those aircraft. Coordinated textiles, color schemes and environmental graphics were deployed throughout the Braniff branding. Attendants received fashionable, of-the-moment uniforms that complemented the interior design of each aircraft.

Figure 3.7
Chief purser and Braniff hostesses in first class section of a Boeing 747. Braniff Airways Collection, History of Aviation Collection, Special Collections and Archives Division, Eugene. McDermott Library, The University of Texas at Dallas

Travelers were welcomed to a new forward-looking future as soon as they entered the Braniff lounges in the airport and were totally immersed in an impeccably designed interior during their flight. Use of bright, bold color schemes, psychedelic patterns, and large-scale interior applications were new and exciting to travelers of the day, who were used to neutral, durable palettes, muted interiors, and a conservative business-like aesthetic. Braniff presented an image of a fun-filled, highly designed, ambitious, placeless future—and travelers loved it.

Figure 3.8
Entrance Hall C of Braniff at Love Field Airport by Alexander Girard. Braniff Airways Collection, History of Aviation Collection, Special Collections and Archives Division, Eugene. McDermott Library, The University of Texas at Dallas.

Braniff's rebranding proposed a counter to the idea of the open road that positioned travel as an experience in and of itself. The placeless experience of travel in these immersive, choreographed environments created their own sense of journey as the destination. Much like film sets and retail displays, Braniff offered a new untethered experience of space that laid the groundwork for people to imagine a shared global future.

The Bianca Cruise Ferry, designed by Atelier Manferdini in 2012, is a pleasure cruise meant for the leisure class to travel and experience new environments mediated by the specifically designed interior space of the ferry. Situated on Japan's Lake Biwa, the vessel gives us a contemporary version of Braniff Airlines' immersive travel experience. In this case, though, that experience is made more complex through careful deployment of reflectivity, color, and view, producing an alternate experience of Lake Biwa only perceived within this ferry's particular interior.

Manferdini utilizes a mostly white and black material palette to neutralize the vertical elements, walls, and furnishings in the space in order to prioritize the horizon and the perceived expansiveness of the

Figure 3.9
Bianca ferry. Photo courtesy of Atelier Manferdini, 2012

Figure 3.10
Bianca ferry. Photo courtesy of Atelier Manferdini, 2012

Figure 3.11
Bianca ferry. Photo courtesy of Atelier Manferdini, 2012

interior into the landscape. Windows are left uncovered, wrapping the interior in colorful views of the exterior foliage and lake during the day and layering reflections at night. When the sun goes down, lights on the shore are mirrored by reflections in the lake's water and both are veiled by reflections of the ferry's interior activities in the glass of the windows. This serene condition of being in a boat on the lake is reiterated by the designer's careful articulation of soft, shiny color and mirrored material in the ferry's ceilings.

Manferdini created patterns for the ceilings that draw from the colors of the lake and its surrounding foliage over the course of the day (ateliermanferdini.com, 2016). The ferry's interior design focuses our experience in the ferry to a precise moment of being on the lake. The shininess of the ceiling creates a similarly layered condition; it reflects the views of the exterior coupled with the activity of people reflected up from the inside, melding with the various color palettes and visually expanding our experience of being inside on the lake together.

The faceted, elongated patterns in the ceilings and floors expand our perspectival experience beyond the physical confines of the ferry and accentuate an extended, limitless interior/exterior experience. The patterns inspire flows of movement within the ferry that connect to the motion of the vessel on the water, the flows of change over the course of the day, and change across seasons. One could ride this ferry many times without repeating the same experience. Manferdini's Bianca ferry acts as a transformational device, transitioning and collapsing the exterior landscape on to a shared interior activity at a given moment.

PUBLIC TRANSIT, INCLUSIVENESS AND NATIONAL IDENTITY

London has led the world in public transit systems. From the underground "Tube" system to its extensive bus network, the city has for many generations prioritized and exemplified excellent public transit facilities. Here, we will specifically chronicle the iconic red London bus. In the 1930s the London Transport Executive was formed and tasked with systematizing a vast network of private transit vehicles. At the time there were 42 different bus models in use, and London Transport made it a priority to advance the system through an unprecedented investment in a new bus design (*The Routemaster Bus,* BBC documentary, 1992).

In the mid-1950s LT's Routemaster double-decker bus model was introduced. Teams of engineers and designers developed the Routemaster, with the styling led by Douglas Scott. This new model included hydro brakes and independent springs for a more comfortable ride, automatic transmission and, notably, fresh air heating. Heating of this sort was not widely available even in privately owned cars of the time, yet it was considered a worthwhile luxury to provide to the general public. New lightweight materials such as aluminum and

Figure 3.12
Routemaster interior. Photo: Simon Pielow

glass fiber were deployed in modular panels designed to keep the overall weight down, allowing for a slightly larger bus to increase passenger capacity. The paneled design also provided easy access to internal parts and the ability to clean and maintain the vehicles quickly and frequently. The two-level "double-decker" design was carried forward into the Routemaster from an earlier, commonly used, horse-drawn stagecoach design that used a spiral stair at the back to double capacity. The design of the Routemaster assumed a two-person crew: a driver at the front where the engine was housed and a conductor at the back to man the entrance, collect tickets, and offer directions and anecdotes about London to passengers. The interior design of the bus carefully considered both of these roles. A driving cockpit was designed with the driver's operational needs in mind, and a standing cubby embedded under the stairs provided the conductor with a place to stand away from the flow of passenger traffic entering and exiting the bus. Moquette fabrics for the passenger seats were designed with a bold checkered pattern in various shades of red and light green. Bright yellow stripes ran vertically through the pattern to maintain a fresh appearance over time as the fabric wore with use.

When production of the Routemaster was stopped in 1968, new but decidedly lesser off-the-shelf models were introduced that housed the engine at the back of the bus and the entrance at the front. This allowed the driver to also collect fares, eventually doing away with the conductor.

Figure 3.13
New London Bus, exterior view. London Transport, 2012

By 2012, after more than 50 years of constant use, the Routemaster model was retired in London. Many of the buses were sold to municipalities around the world and are still in use. London Transport renewed its commitment to iconic, accessible, and excellent design for the public good by engaging the designer Thomas Heatherwick to produce what was originally referred to as a New Bus for London. Heatherwick maintained much of the original ethos of the design agenda: to provide convenient transport in the capital while maintaining the London bus's status as a globally recognized mobile monument. His new design successfully manages a preservationist fascination with the original Routemaster while introducing a number of modern innovations and more universally accessible features.

The New Bus for London is still iconically red and maintains two levels. Heatherwick Studio kept the front entrance, added an entrance in the middle of the bus, and reintroduced the rear entrance platform. This new bus is three meters longer than the original Routemaster, making for higher passenger capacity while also providing space for the extra doors. The three-entrance design allows passengers to enter and exit more efficiently, allowing each route to match modern demands for speedier service. "Protruding lumps of machinery encased in mysterious fiber-glass housings" (heatherwick.com, 2016) are relocated to preference a clean, streamlined interior in the New Bus design.

Figure 3.14
New London Bus, interior view. Photo: Tony Duell, 2013

The New Bus also has two sets of stairs to access the upper deck. Windows are redesigned from the inside out, following the angle of the stairs to provide unhindered views of London while sitting in or moving around the bus. At the front entrance the window tilts down to allow the driver to easily see small children and wheelchair-bound passengers. These sweeping windows are one of the most identifiable aspects of the New Bus, paired with a curved exterior to lessen the perceived mass of the new, larger model. The upper deck provides a mobile view of London unequaled by walking through the streets or riding in a car.

The interior finishes and color palette acknowledge the immense wear each bus sustains. With buses being cleaned only once a day in a mostly wet climate, Heatherwick considered every surface material and finish carefully. Floors are a dark grey, made more visually durable with a slight pattern to camouflage passenger spills and muddy, salty stains during the rainy seasons. Upper surfaces that are more rarely touched are white and shiny to perceptibly lift the space and make it feel brighter and bigger. Natural light during the day is abundant through the many windows and bounces off the ceiling surface, evenly illuminating the space. Warm artificial lighting is embedded in the ceiling to provide ease of navigation at night without producing unwanted harsh glares or reflections in the windows. Especially on the second floor, this careful attention to the ceiling light helps passengers to focus on the view of London.

Seats maintain the classic moquette fabric, with a new digitally modified checkered pattern. Again, checkered bright lines contrast tones of red—only here the pattern and lines warp to the contours of the human body associated with the surfaces of the seat. The distortion masks stains and wear. Throughout the interior, Bright pops of color are used sparingly to draw attention to stop signals and hand supports for stability while

Figure 3.15
New London Bus, interior view of the stairs. Photo: David Holt

the bus is in motion. Hand supports are offered in multiple locations and configurations to maximize accessibility for a variety of body types and abilities.

What is most significant about this New Bus for London is its powerful design, one that produces a mobile monument of iconic London that anyone can access and which serves an active, modern public. The New Bus for London provides a point of pride in both its iconic red exterior and a shared experience of the city via the interior for tourists and those who use it daily. Riding the New Bus for London is still an essential and monumental experience when visiting London

Figure 3.16
Moquette fabric, New London Bus. Photo: Camira Fabrics

CONCLUSION

These three case studies highlight the many roles interior design plays in forming and reinforcing shared values towards environmental resources and protected landscapes, diverse human experiences in space, and cultural identity. As this volume seeks to blur and expand the disciplinary terrain that interior design effects, these mobile interiors provide a clear focus for disciplinary expertise anchored in the precise and complex understanding of varied forms of human habitation in spaces designed for mobility.

SECTION III

THE AUTONOMOUS INSIDE

The autonomy of the interior offers the possibility for alternate aesthetic or sensory experiences that challenge the way we inhabit the world. Free from uncontrolled variations in climate and context, inhabitable art pieces, stage sets, merchandising displays, and infrastructural conditions allow us to inhabit at times fantastical realities. They offer new spatial experiences that challenge the confines of traditional programmatic elements, typical code requirements or other pragmatic limitations. These interiors have the unique ability to delight and surprise us, changing environmental expectations through this distinct condition of contextual independence.

PROVOCATIONS:

- Can autonomous interiors narrate their own context?
- Can sequenced interiors operate as a networked infrastructural system independent of its enclosed context?
- How does inhabitable space dictate personal and social behavior? How do personal and social behaviors dictate inhabitable space?

04 Artists occupying interiors occupying artists

Alex Schweder

No matter his or her medium, every artist creates an interior, a subjective experience inside the minds of the audience. Within the context of this publication, suggesting that the expertise of producing interior space is also in the purview of a discipline other than interior design may read as an affront to some. This provocation, however, is meant to enrich the field of interior design, not dilute it. Through the artworks featured in this chapter, three of which I co-created, I will argue that the interior qualities of designed environments are so imbricated with the interior subjectivities of their occupants that it is not possible to discuss the interior of a building without also addressing the psychological interiors of the inhabitants. Interiors are made from both subjectivity and sofas, and designers not only have legitimacy in working with both but they can be as playful with behavior as they have become with bricks.

In studying spaces that artists design and occupy, this chapter will show that not only are interiors expressions of their inhabitants' identities, struggles, and relationships, but they produce them as well. To map the relationship between interior space and inhabitant as suggested, it is useful to see how artists forged a similar path in their field. By tracing how the subjectivity of artistic audiences came to be constituted as the art itself, I will argue that the same relationship that exists between performance art and audience also exists between inhabited space and inhabitant.

Historically, visitors to museums were thought to passively receive meaning emanating from a painting or sculpture[1] (Hill, 2003: 22), thus locating the value of the work in the material object itself rather than its impact on viewers. Frustrated by the reduction of their work to a commodity, artists working in the mid-twentieth century began shifting the definition of art away from marketable objects toward ineffable subjective experiences. As a strategy toward this end, artists recast viewers of their works from passive consumers into collaborative producers whose perception of an artwork produced the meaning. As part of this change, artists began making immersive environments that stimulated the full sensorium of their visitors' bodies.

Artists who make interiors today heighten the perception of their audiences by breaking their habituated ways of using spaces, often riffing on the everyday environments that interior designers produce. These artists identify their trope as "installation art." While their palettes overlap with interior design through the use of materials, scale, and the reconfiguration of existing spaces, a key difference between installation art and interior design is how each discipline thinks about occupants. Where interior designers might ask: "How does this environment reflect who my client is?", an installation artist might ask: "Who will a person become when entering the space I make?" One question characterizes a subject's psychological interior as static, while the latter understands subjectivity as plastic. It is because of their allowance for fluidity in subjectivity that I choose to reference artistic endeavors rather than engage the history of design, which contains prevalent and problematic attitudes towards behavior evidenced in movements such as functionalism.

To explore the idea that corporeal occupation of an interior space can beget psychological transformation, performance artists have lived for several days or even weeks in environments they built. From the late twentieth century, Chris Burden's *Five Day Locker Piece* (1971)[2], Vito Acconci's *Seed Bed* (1971)[3], or Linda Montano and Tehching Hsieh's *Cage Piece* (1978–79)[4] are a few such historical precedents. Artists today build on such works by constructing and occupying extreme interiors and using them as giant microscopes through which they can more clearly see how these environments influence their subjectivities.

Sometimes, however, an artist's planned outcome and what actually happens during a performance do not align. Marcel Duchamp spoke of this in 1957 as the "art coefficient" (Lebel, 1959: 77–78), referring to this gap between artistic intention and its reception. Here, Duchamp claims, is where creativity and art occur, in the space where clear communication between people breaks down and interpretation is used to construct a makeshift bridge over the chasm of possible meanings. In the performance artworks that I will be discussing, the authors occupy their works with the intention of the space precipitating a psychic transformation. The only people who can verify if the intended change in subjectivity occurs, however, are the artists themselves. This puts them in the awkward position of acknowledging that a work did not actualize their pre-inhabitation hopes if something unexpected occurred. Duchamp's theory is perhaps most helpful in this moment, when the person that the artist wanted to become and what they actually became are not the same thing. Duchamp's position gives artists a way around the idea that living in their work is a failure if the result is different from the point of departure intention. Duchamp's theory affirms that the most creative moments are produced by the unknown and unexpected.

To explore the connection between subjective alteration and spatial inhabitation I will discuss six artworks in this chapter: three from the practices of other artists and three from my own. While I can only corroborate what I experienced, discussing the three initial works will provide a context for the latter, which have similar practices and ambitions.

THE HOUSE WITH THE OCEAN VIEW

In 2002 Marina Abramović, whose seminal performance art spans decades, lived in *The House with the Ocean View* between November 15 and 26 at Sean Kelly, a gallery in New York City. Her artistic intent was to endure the stresses of a 12-day occupation of an interior comprised of only three sparsely furnished rooms suspended above the gallery floor; one for sleeping, one for sitting and one for ablution. She only consumed water, never spoke to the audience, and performed every action —including bathing and urinating—in front of her audience. Abramović describes the set up as ritualized fasting using the repetition of both everyday actions and a metronome to induce a trance-like state wherein she is "purified." While purification is a slippery term in this context (Birringer, 2003),[5] it does suggest the artist's desire to influence her subjectivity through occupation of an interior space. By continuously living in this ascetic interior, I interpret that she wished to become as empty as her environment.

What Abramović filled herself up with are the silent connections she has with her audience. As the title of the work suggests, the artist considered her audience from the very start; the mass of their presence was the "ocean." Throughout the work she singled out members of her audience (as she would come to do again a decade later in her performance of *The Artist is Present*), and in silence they would "exchange energy," as the artist described it. According to the artist, a connection between them was made that could not have come about if they were in a more distracted state. For Abramović, empathy and connection are facilitated by space and circumstance; so in an adjacent room there was a bed and costume that a member of the audience could occupy for one hour to become more like the artist. From this set up I speculate that Abramović's intention for her and her audience's subjectivity was to transform mental experience into something shared, and that her vehicle to do so was the interior occupied by both.

DANS LA PEAU DE L'OURS

French artist Abraham Poincheval also used physical deprivation to induce mental alteration in his 2014 occupation performance *Dans la peau de l'ours* (In the bear's skin). Poincheval, in his own words,[6] wanted to become more "bear like." To induce the hibernation associated with this animal, Poincheval lived in the interior of a bear sculpture that he fabricated using a wooden formwork. Without leaving this womb-like space for 13 days, he slept, read, and lived his life in what looked like a taxidermy bear on the outside and a Tom Sachs[7] spaceship on the inside. Before beginning the performance Poincheval had loaded up one leg with the food he thought a bear might eat (honey, berries, and the like), designed a second leg to supply water and collect urine, a third leg collected trash, and the final leg let in fresh air. Almost as a photo-negative of Abramović's relationship with her audience, Poincheval's audience could not see him but were encouraged to chat with him to keep him company. Even though the somatic artist/audience exchanges were different, both relied on the interior spaces[8] of exhibition and inhabitation to precipitate psychic change.

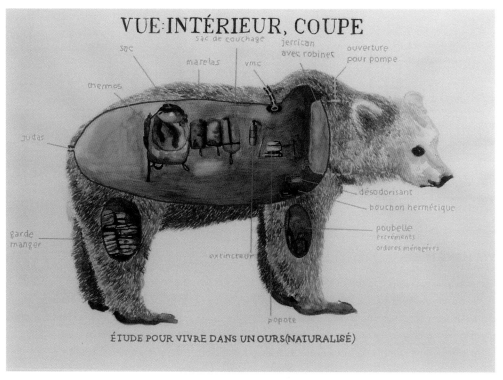

Figure 4.1

Étude pour vivre dans un ours (naturalisé) vue extérieure. Abraham Poincheval. © Collection Musée Gassendi, Digne-les-Bains

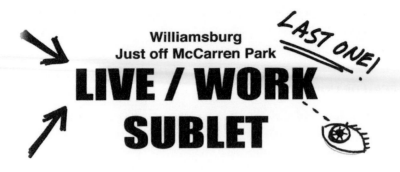

Figure 4.2
We Have Mice, Ward Shelley, 2004

WE HAVE MICE

"Becoming animal" was also the point of departure for a third interior inhabitation, by artist Ward Shelley in 2004 when he lived mouse-like in the walls of Pierogi Gallery (then located in New York's emergently trendy Williamsburg neighborhood). His occupation of the gallery's poché was a metaphor for the plight of artists in the neighborhood, and only unexpectedly did his occupation induce a shift in subjectivity. Mice in the company of humans, for Shelley, are the less powerful creatures and are thus forced to occupy the periphery of a space, just as the artists who moved into the neighborhood in the 1990s were being forced to do because of gentrification. Initially intended to be a one-month performance and occupation, Shelley left only to "forage for food, materials and mating opportunities." (Cotter, 2004). Shelley's interactions were quite different from those of either Abramović or Poincheval. As it would be for a mouse, evidence of his occupation would emerge obliquely through "droppings." In Shelley's case these were notecards featuring artwork that he made while living within the gallery walls and slid through slits cut in the gypsum board. These pieces of paper were inscribed with sayings such as "Self-critique just isn't sexy, I don't know why," or "I'm judging you too."

Figure 4.3
We Have Mice, Ward Shelley, 2004

Figure 4.4
We Have Mice, Ward Shelley, 2004

We Have Mice was written up in several high-profile publications, including *The New York Times*. Accolades like these padded the artist's psychological interior against the stress normally experienced when inhabiting an extreme physical interior, until the exhibition was extended for a week. He recounted[9] how he experienced a psychic break after the performance unexpectedly went beyond its anticipated duration. This change felt like a loss of autonomy, and Shelley reported that his burrow began to feel like a detention cell. Caged animal-like behaviors followed. He said he started acting irrationally and even broke up with a girlfriend. When he finally exited the work and went home to his own studio, his home, ironically, had been taken over by rats.

Did Poincheval feel more bearish or Abramović more pure? Is the work a failure if these things never happen or if some entirely other psychological interior occurs, as was admitted by Shelley in the *Mice* performance? Can we consider the unintended push back of an interior to be its own kind of subjectivity, independent of its occupants? These are the questions that I will consider for the remainder of this chapter as I discuss first-hand accounts of my own collaborations with Shelley where we were both authors and audience.

FLATLAND, STABILITY, AND IN ORBIT

Shelley and I met as Fellows at the American Academy in Rome in 2005. During the year we spent together there my own emergent ideas on performance and architecture were finding expression. I shared my view that architecture has always contained performances, and we discussed Shelley's works in which the performance of daily routine influenced the shape the architecture took over time.

In 2007 Shelley and I synthesized these ideas through a project called *Flatland*, inspired by the Edwin Abbott novella of the same name in which characters inhabit a two-dimensional world.

Winston Churchill's phrase, "We shape our buildings and, afterwards, our buildings shape us,"[10] influenced my thinking about how buildings change the ways in which we behave. I was curious about how an extreme interior environment would affect me, my relationships with other artists, and my relationship with the building itself.

At New York's Sculpture Center we constructed a structure that was as close to two dimensions as we could make it. Abbott's inhabitants of Flatland had a radically different understanding of a world in which only two dimensions were perceived; we wanted to experience a similar shift. Our building was four storeys tall, 24 feet wide and two feet deep. Six of us[11] committed to occupying the structure for three weeks, with the only rule being "you can leave at any time but you cannot re-enter." My fantasy at the beginning of this work was that we would quickly change the building in reaction to a space that constrained us.

What actually happened was quite different. Because our building's dimensions were so confining, assembling our entire community in one location was impossible. Our early interactions were limited to two-person encounters. Confined within two feet, an occupant was only ever able to face and talk to one flatmate at a time. There was never the opportunity to have a group discussion, because we could only meet in a line. Issues could not easily be addressed as a community and our group of six began to form associations divided by two personality types, which I will call the "order people" and "free-spirit people." Those who normally thrived in the clamor of many people and things simultaneously vying for their attention seemed to find the space frustrating. Easily distracted, they tended to generate (in the eyes of this "order person") chaos and clutter in the shared 196 square-foot space that the three "order people" found problematic. Because broad communication was thwarted by the shape of the interior space, differences in style led to misunderstandings

Figure 4.5
Flatland, Alex Schweder and Ward Shelley, 2007. Photo: Mark Linz

Figure 4.6
Flatland, Alex Schweder and Ward Shelley, 2007. Photo: Mark Linz

and defensiveness. Those who preferred more internal stimulation became withdrawn and, by the two-week mark, the "free-spirits" had elected to leave—not so much due to the social polarization as the space's inability to afford group conversations. By the end of *Flatland* the three of us remaining were working happily in our two-by-eight feet rooms. The vacated spaces were left empty. We had adapted to the environment by taking on tasks that were inward and contained; hibernating in a way, similar to Poincheval.

While conceptualizing this work with Shelley I had conveyed to him my expectations of how the physical form of the building would change over time. I thought that the building would come to look like an old shoe, portions of its envelope stretched and worn from the internal forces of its occupation. The space was, in fact, too restrictive for any of us to feel we could alter the structure. If one person were to saw some wood, the dust would fall into the bedroom below. Every movement required careful planning. My desire to make a building whose form changed in direct relation to occupation remained unfulfilled. In retrospect, however, this project's success for me was the realization that architecture could be practiced solely by working with the subjectivity of its users.

Precisely because this project's outcome did not align with my initial expectations, the observations made during, and reflections arising from, the experience of performing *Flatland* generated new ideas for future performances. *Flatland* clarified my desire to make an environment that changed physically in direct relation to its occupation in order to visualize the intersubjectivity that it was producing.

In pursuit of this ambition Shelley and I began designing a new situation to inhabit in 2009, *Stability*. Suspended at its center, tilting one way or the other like a seesaw in reaction to the occupants' location, the relationship of the two inhabitants to one another was immediately visible through the building's incline. If one of us moved away from the fulcrum and the other did not, the angle of the building would change, impacting on the other's experience of the space. The other person would have to either move in order to re-level the space or continue what they were doing at an angle. In this way it was like an "occupant-harmony-o-meter," where viewers could gauge our willingness to cooperate through the tilt of the floor.

Like *Flatland*, this work can be considered an architectural caricature, a building that exaggerates something already occurring in and through designed spaces—namely, the construction of relationships between inhabitants as affected by the spaces they occupy. Such changes to our subjectivity become habituated and we no longer realize they are occurring. Yet typical multi-family housing affects who we are, how we behave, and our perception of our neighbors. If the walls allow sounds to permeate from the adjoining flat we find ourselves changing how we use the space.

Shelley and I occupied *Stability* for nine days. By the end we had become constantly, but unconsciously, aware of one another's activities. We had adapted to the initial frustrations we encountered, and in a sense our experience of this space had become domesticated. Thus, in a sort of "domestic bliss," Shelley and I came to know what the other was feeling through the building. Slight shifts in weight coming with more frequency often signaled agitation with work or other relationships. There was never a need to knock because the building would tip in anticipation of approach. Our scale-like structure was not just visualizing intersubjectivity but producing it.

Through the extreme situations that *Flatland* and *Stability* set up, Shelley and I gained an intimate understanding of how buildings influence our subjectivity. In both of these inhabitations our relationship to one another through the building was optional; we could always opt out of it. By the end of both of these projects we thought that their dimensional anomaly, width, and incline were too quickly adapted to. *Flatland* should have been thinner and *Stability* should have had a 30-degree, rather than a 15-degree, tilt.

In 2014 we found an opportunity to make a work where cooperation through tandem living was non-negotiable. Through Shelley's relationship with Pierogi we built and performed *In Orbit*, a 25-feet wheel that Shelley and I lived on continuously for ten days. Furniture for six activities was affixed to the interior and exterior of the wheel: bathing, dressing, cooking, working, relaxing, and sleeping. To change activities we would need to coordinate not only our schedules but also our locomotion to turn the entire wheel until the desired furniture rotated toward us.

Figure 4.7

Stability, Alex Schweder and Ward Shelley, 2009. Photo: Alex Schweder and Ward Shelley

Figure 4.8

In Orbit, Alex Schweder and Ward Shelley, 2014. Photo: Scott Lynch

Figure 4.9
In Orbit, Alex Schweder and Ward Shelley, 2014. Photo: Scott Lynch

While our intent was to set up equitable living spaces, we soon found that Shelley's experience on the top of the wheel was quite different from mine. Occupying a concave floor versus a convex one makes for an appreciable difference in how quotidian tasks can be managed. I was able to take my shoes off at night and put them on the floor next to my bed, for example, while Shelley would need to tether his up to prevent them falling off the wheel's circumference. He was more likely to fall than I was and thereby needed to spend the duration of the performance harnessed with a safety line to one of the metal beams above. He depended on me to act responsibly to prevent bodily harm, since my body was providing the weight that kept the wheel from rotating unexpectedly. Emotionally, Shelley expressed difficulty in having to inconvenience me. He described his experience as akin to being a car passenger needing to make a stop, whether for a stretch, toilet break, or for food. The passenger, he described, is at a disadvantage and feels as though he is under the driver's control. This fundamental power imbalance requires that the passenger trusts the driver not to abuse control. Shelley recognized that these recurring feelings, prompted by the architectural circumstance we had contrived, were in fact rooted in his own psychological make-up.

Again, we intended something other than what we experienced—coordination and dependence respectively. Over several projects Shelley and I have come to understand that this disconnect is productive of new work. As I write we are using the unexpected experience of caretaking to inform a new work titled *Dead*

Man Friend.[12] In this new performance, after a coin flip one of us will sacrifice his autonomy so that the other can thrive. Again, we will use an interior space to manifest this complex relationship. The work will comprise a fully programmed apartment with a workspace, sleeping area, kitchen, and bathroom that one of us occupies. The one who sacrifices his autonomy will stay only in a bed for the duration of the performance. The bed will be situated, either through ropes or balance, such that if the artist in the bed gets up then the other artist's dwelling will fall apart. In return, the artist whose house is held up through sacrifice needs to tend to the artist in bed by feeding him, changing his bed pan, cleaning him and keeping him company. Each contingent to the other in different ways; caretaking, when necessitated by the design of a habitable space, makes the complexity of the relationship palpable.

CONCLUSION

Practicing designers are not known for embracing uncertainty. The preparation and coordination required to ensure a project is within budget and on schedule prohibit many designers from leaving much to chance. As we have seen through the environments designed by and lived in by artists, the unknown is the human subject and who they will become through the space. This aspect of design, who we will become in relation to it, is an emergent area of spatial aesthetics. Considering the formation of subjectivity in relation to occupation no doubt has its pitfalls if a designer applies the same control over a subject as they do over objects. If, though, designers can work with occupants to use their spaces in innovative and playful ways, the latter gains a sense of agency and self-determination.

NOTES

01 Hill citing W. Benjamin's *The Work of Art.*
02 In his final year at University of California, Irvine, Chris Burden lived in one of the school's lockers for five days, with only five gallons of water located in the locker above and an empty five-gallon container in the locker below.
03 Reconfiguring the floor of the Sonnabend Gallery in New York to slope upward and create an inhabitable space below it, Acconci would spend the day in this cavity masturbating to fantasies based on the unseen movements of the visitors above him.
04 Montano and Hsieh lived for one year in New York City tied together by a rope around their waists that only allowed them to be eight feet apart. They went about their lives as best they could.
05 Here Birringer acknowledges the ease by which this work's notion of purity can be undermined as glibly assuming uncritical new age spirituality.
06 GeoBeats News, April 2 2014, www.youtube.com/watch?v=L29Qd3vtoV8.
07 Sachs is a contemporary American artist, born in 1966, who roughly assembles quotidian materials, such as wood and Tyvek, to make approximations of highly technical objects such as the Apollo lunar module.
08 This performance was staged at Le Musée de la Chasse et de la Nature (the Museum of Hunting) in Paris, located in two combined historic buildings from the seventeenth and eighteenth centuries. As its mission the museum "exhibits the relationships between humans and animals from antiquity to today." The rooms of this building are themed by animal, and contain objects that have been used to communicate, hunt, and culturally contextualize the animal of focus, from poems to whistles and primitive portraits to contemporary art. When walking through the museum's rooms, visitors sense what it is like to become animal. Poincheval's performance furthered the museum's subtly executed mission by enacting it in an extreme way.
09 Ward Shelley, in discussion with the author, March 21, 2016.
10 On October 28, 1943 Winston Churchill was addressing the British House of Commons in the House of Lords to consider the reconstruction of the former after its 1941 destruction by the Germans. The debate was between rebuilding the old design that did not have enough seats for all members or constructing a new design with ample

space. Churchill successfully argued for reconstruction by pointing out that the cramped feeling of a too-small space embodied the importance of a decision when all members were in attendance.

11 The other four artists participating in the *Flatland* performance were Pelle Brage, Eva LaCour, Douglas Paulson, and Maria Petsching.

12 In building construction, a "dead man" refers to a mass buried underground that acts as an anchor for a structural element that is in tension. *Dead Man* was also the title of Chris Burden's 1972 performance where he pretended to be a corpse next to a car on the highway. *Dead Man Friend* simultaneously refers to both of these while also implying a relationship.

05   Interiors for display and on display

Karin Tehve

> Each in its sphere attempts to combine the interest in duration, unity and similarity with that in change, specialization and peculiarity. It becomes self-evident that there is no institution, no law, no estate of life, which can uniformly satisfy the full demands of the two opposing principles.
>
> (Simmel 1957: 542)

Display is a curious word. Its Latin ancestor, *displicāre*, meant to scatter or disperse[1], at first glance antonymous to the collection of things inherent to exhibition. Neither does this root speak to the careful sequencing, housing, and framing that is part of display's core program.

It is a verb as well as a noun, which speaks to the active, fluid aspects of its contemporary nature. Its active sense also suggests an end (something displayed is seen) as well as a means; in the case studies described in this text, contemporary interiors for display propose a very visible infrastructure, active in the construction of display as a point of exchange. The interiors described in the case studies mediate people and things at an accelerating temporal scale at odds with both the assumption that constructed environments are fixed or that sharp distinctions can be drawn between types of interiors for display.

In his essay *Fashion*, Georg Simmel describes our dual drives for permanence and novelty, an essential opposition fundamental to one's nature and to understanding much of social interaction and material production. Simmel discusses fashion broadly as both an attraction to difference (something new) and similarity (belonging). Each movement or trend contains within itself *a simultaneous beginning and end* (Simmel 1957: 547), and that it is the acknowledgement of the fashionable object or praxis' transitoriness that is a large part of its attraction. Simmel's fashion is analogous to the temporal scales mediated by interiors for display.

Display as a program concerns a heterogeneous typology, encompassing galleries, museums, trade shows and retail in its myriad manifestations. At first glance vastly different in terms of their cultural roles, it is worth noting that the contemporary museum and department store developed almost simultaneously. The 1870s saw the origins of an astonishing number of familiar, long-standing institutions: the construction of the Philadelphia Museum of Art as well as John Wanamaker's Grand Depot department store, the construction and expansion of the Museum of Natural History in New York with a similar time-line for Macy's department store. The same decade saw the establishment of the Metropolitan Museum of Art in New York and the construction of Eiffel's Bon Marché in Paris.

Display programs together took advantage of the modern mobility of women (newly scattered and dispersed at the end of the nineteenth century) and helped steer the traditional Sunday promenade from a public ritual on urban sidewalks into an interior pursuit (Gunn 1999; 122). The promenade (the word itself an activity and a kind of place) was ostensibly a walk for recreational purposes, but was also a form of social intercourse. This walk was normally undertaken in order to see and be seen by neighbors and acquaintances. The interior promenade experience continued to perform the program of self-display while functioning as the ostensible rationale for the institutional visit; this gave hosting institutions an audience as well.

Museums and department stores continue to share many idioms of display deployed at their conceptions and that remain in heavy rotation today, with striking similarities at the point of contact with the visitor or consumer. The shop window has its parallel in the diorama, and each variant above makes liberal use of vitrines, platforms, and similar case-work.

These containers structure taxonomies of collections or stock, protect the valuable (whether through workmanship, rarity or brand), and set artifacts apart, creating a focused space between viewers and things (whether for the long term or the short). They create visual and experiential unities of collections that are in flux, adapting to new research, acquisitions, cultural values, ontological conditions, or seasons regularly. It is this scale of the environment that turned the promenade into browsing, and yet these forms are so familiar as to be rendered invisible in the little attention paid to them. Marshall McLuhan suggested that anything used to transmit content—an idea, an image, a message, or a brand—is a form of media (McLuhan 1999: 8). In this case the display infrastructure itself performs that function, without necessarily drawing any notice.

This armature also mediates the permanence of the institution (*duration, unity, and similarity*) and the experience of its changing collections of artifacts (*change, specialization, and peculiarity*), the core of the user's experience. In this model the artifacts to be experienced themselves can exist at an impermanent extreme, case-work and fitting quickly modified to house them. The closest kin to display assemblies may be stage sets, the architectural enclosure that houses them arbitrary vis-à-vis its dramatic content and both framing and enabling the performance of the exchange itself.

Museums as institutions confer durable cultural value to their collections, but are seen as imposing and exclusive by much of the public. Retail is a critical mediator in the flow of goods and economic capital, but its commercial identity imposes a ceiling on its high-cultural influence. McLuhan posited it was the form rather than the content of media that *shaped the scale and form of human association* (McLuhan 1999: 9); if interiors for display function like media they would help blur distinctions between the programs that utilize them in the minds of visitors/consumers. These blurs are available for any of the display programs to exploit to their advantage (to enact accessibility or imply the creation of cultural capital); and, indeed, the speed of change and the overlaps between institutions remain on upward trajectories.

In 1998 B. Joseph Pine II and James Gilmore published an article in the *Harvard Business Review* entitled "Welcome to the Experience Economy." This oft-quoted text suggests that the next basis for the economy (from agrarian to goods to services) would now be *experiences*; that, for businesses or institutions to be successful, the focus should be on the visitor's or customer's memories of the exchange, not the artifacts themselves. Proposed in the context of the essay as a paradigmatic shift, it is an evolution of the promenade becoming an interior pursuit. Since then, market research continues to tell us that the middle-class and upper-middle-class consumer is driven by a desire for "exclusive locations [and] rare and unusual experiences" (trendwatching.com 2016). Exclusivity (a strategy tied to perceived or actual value) is often now a function of space *and* time, some delight offered up for a limited time (and sometimes made known only to a select few). The accommodations for this programming (special programs or events, visiting exhibitions, pop-ups) have helped further support Simmel's assertions regarding the desire for permanence and novelty within the same phenomenon (Simmel 1957: 547) and further foreground the components of interior display as the mediating element. Not only do the artifacts to be experienced change, but the larger context in which they are experienced changes too. These strategies have become commonplace across display programs, and they continue to borrow liberally from one another.

Perhaps the most extensive and best published of these strategies can be seen through the collaboration between the Italian fashion house Prada and the Office for Metropolitan Architecture (OMA), a Dutch architectural firm, and its research office AMO.

OMA has designed a number of "permanent" environments for Prada; the best known in the US are the Epicenters (in New York, Los Angeles, and San Francisco), akin to flagship stores. The Epicenters house cultural programming and exhibitions, integrated into the retail spaces. The mechanisms for event programming integrated into their interiors are based largely on recognizable display idioms, although occasionally newly mobile—platforms, case-work and vitrines. Both OMA and AMO have designed pop-up and event programming at a range of scales for Prada and Miu Miu (a sister brand): from catwalks for fashion shows (up to and including the men's fall collection, shown in spring of 2016) to a pop-up museum (in January 2012, with Italian artist Francesco Vezzoli) existing for only one day (designboom.com 2012). While blending programming from across display program typologies, OMA's containers are rarely gallery-neutral. These temporary interior elements assert a visible and active presence to create distinctive temporary atmospheres for the duration of an event.

To propose case-studies primarily of pop-up programs for display is perhaps over-determined, given the hypothesis, but these pop-ups embrace their temporary nature with tenacity. The following examples all utilize a blur: between typological distinctions, definable form versus immateriality, permanence versus novelty. Each was further selected for the ability to create a strongly defined interior space independent of the qualities of its enclosing architecture; while most use idioms prototypical of a conventional interior for display, these details are deployed in ways to highlight this independence and to find new modes of expression therein.

FOAM/FABRIC

We might consider caves to be interior design's primitive hut, the first enclosure in which we took shelter. The two following projects both feature strong cave-like interior form, yet are constructed of lightweight materials; each could be understood to reference an origin myth while reveling in their own temporary states. The New York design firm Snarkitecture worked with fashion designer Richard Chai to create a pop-up for the designer's collection as part of the BOFFO Building Fashion[2] series in 2010; the site was an existing modified shipping container provided by BOFFO under the High Line, the context already forming a powerful interiority. Hand-cut foam was used to create a liner and all-display infrastructure; indeed, all surfaces but for small clear areas of floor and ceiling. While the foam is white, an easy comparison to a white-box gallery would have to stop there. The foam is carved to accommodate niches for hanging clothing, or ledges for accessories. Its visual analogs toy with opposing time scales. From a distance the foam resembles snow, a building material embraced by both children and northern nomadic tribes for its availability, affordability, and low environmental impact, its temporary nature acknowledged. The cut edges as seen from the container's glazed end reinforce this reading, both through its irregular faceted forms and the apparently arbitrary end condition vis-à-vis its shell, cut or pressed like a drift against a window. Although planned for a very limited duration, one can imagine repeated sessions of carving over time, to erase unwanted marks of wear, accommodate new collections, or simply delight in seeing those forms melt into their enclosing surfaces.

A closer view suggests stone, the material of fixity, stability, and constancy in any of its traditional fabricated states; here the forms recall the slow process of erosion by wind or water—unfixed, but made inconstant by

Figure 5.1
Snarkitecture with Richard Chai, NYC, 2010. Photo: David Smith

Figure 5.2
Snarkitecture with Richard Chai, NYC, 2010. Photo: Snarkitecture

a process sometimes lasting millennia. At the end of the installation the foam was returned to the manufac-
turer and recycled into rigid insulation.

Snarkitecture designed and helped build an installation for the fashion brand COS at Spazio Erbe for
Milan Fashion Week in 2015. The material used was a white synthetic non-woven textile (a reference to the
fashion label's 2015 collection, shown within the installation) suspended from the ceiling and cut into its final
form by the design team. A very materially different palette from the Chai installation, this interior continues
a tension between differing durations. The project's spatial enclosure and materiality also suggest a hybrid
between tent (overall fully three dimensional form) and drape (more fundamentally planar), recalling some
fantastic medieval synthesis.

Like the installation with/for Richard Chai, the overall spatial configuration also recalls a cave, stone operated on by natural forces for millennia, yet its non-fixed nature is called into attention by the daylight, filtered
by the material's translucency, and the movement of the fabric in response to the movement of its visitors
and eddies of warm air created by air flows in this conditioned space.

MIRRORS/SAND

A reflection is that note of color, of light, which contains no form in and of itself, but is pure, shapeless
color. We do not attribute the reflections of a metallic or glazed object to the object itself, as we do its
surface color. The reflection is neither the reflecting object nor whatever may be reflected in it. Instead,
it lies somewhere in between those things, a specter without substance. (Ortega Y Gasset 1990: 187)

Figure 5.3
Office of Neiheiser & Valle with Linda Farrow, New York City, 2013 (exterior). Photo: Linda Farrow

Figure 5.4
Office of Neiheiser & Valle with Linda Farrow, New York City, 2013 (entry). Photo: Linda Farrow

Figure 5.5
Office of Neiheiser & Valle with Linda Farrow, New York City, 2013 (interior). Photo: Linda Farrow

Mirrors are experienced as immaterial. Used expansively, they confound our perception of spatial limits and erase the architectural envelope, a paradoxical invisibility cloak.

In 2013 the Office of Neiheiser & Valle, in collaboration with their client Linda Farrow, designed a pop-up sited in warehouse space at the SuperPier at Hudson River Park in New York City, also part of the BOFFO Building Fashion series. Gravel, deployed within and without the shipping container shell, helps blur the distinctions between the vertical and horizontal as well as the insides and outsides of both physical and virtual reflected volumes. Robert Smithson's work is an easy reference-the formal similarities of the angle/gravel assemblage to Smithson's *Mirror Displacement* series (Smithson notably uses fewer sunglasses) and the pairing of gravel/mirror to his *Mirror* series-but Smithson's pieces do not typically invite the viewer into those mirrored spaces themselves. In the Farrow pop-up, reflections serve not to reproduce the world but to re-present the consumer or visitor and the product as a unity in an endless immersive interior atmosphere, holding the world at bay.

DRAWINGS, 2D AND 3D

Most design proposals involving the constructed environment represent the three-dimensional world in two dimensions, notably through the use of orthographic and projection drawings. These means of representation have been traditionally deployed to project a future physical condition. One might argue that the means of conceiving a spatial project falls into the category of means and methods that encompasses the physical materiality and fabrication of that physical site, but it is uncommon for there to be a blur between

Figure 5.6
Snarkitecture for COS, Los Angeles, 2015. Photo: Noah Kalina

Figure 5.7
Snarkitecture for COS, Los Angeles, 2015. Photo: Noah Kalina

these modes of production. The use of projection drawings in a temporary space proposes its own eternal return, with wit and a minimal material outlay. In 2015 Snarkitecture designed another temporary space for COS featuring the label's 2015 collection. At the site in Austere, a popular event venue in downtown Los Angeles, the space is divided in two by a mirrored wall, its contents organized around the featured colors in that fashion collection: whites and grays, then pinks and warm light browns. Wafer-thin sheet metal panels are suspended from the ceilings, each with a cut-out silhouette of the clothing from the collection forming an aperture. These panels fulfill a wall's function in the subdivision of a larger space, but its material expression refers less to the characteristics of the architectural container than the fashions themselves, in color, disposition and form. The flat sheets can be read like drawings hung in a gallery, destabilizing museum/retail distinctions and lending the clothing an art-like allure.

Figure 5.8
Studio Makkink & Bey for Camper, Lyon, 2012. Photo: Sanchez y Morrow

In 2012 the Dutch designers Studio Makkink & Bey designed a store for shoe brand Camper in Lyon, France. This is the studio's contribution to Camper's Together project (Camper.com 2016), a series of international collaborations between Camper and designers on projects involving both products and interiors.

The designers covered the floors, walls and ceilings of the existing space with drawings of stairs. Elemental three-dimensional stair forms are constructed of paint and plywood. Red lines are painted at each three dimensional juncture, the effect resembling full-scale isometric drawings or of maquettes before typical construction techniques; these display shoes and form benches for visitors to sit on and try the footwear, but the stairs represented on the two-dimensional surfaces project spaces for other, more hypothetical, forms of occupation. These drawn stairs overlap and bend across surfaces like Escher drawings. The drawn-upon surfaces invite users in to complete the space, in their experience of spaces suggested on and well beyond the physical limits of the material envelope. This space is cool, in the way that Marshall McLuhan defines the term, requiring an active participation of the visitor and making a visual pun out of the suggestion that any space for display is a form of media (McLuhan 1999: 23).

DRAWINGS/AIR

Inflatable structures are constructed from widely available and lightweight materials and equipment, often simply plastic sheeting and a fan. Many of the inflatables of the 1960s and 1970s were designed to be temporary and transportable, often built to house gatherings and events, a critique of an inevitable durable constructed environment. The inflatable recently has been repurposed to interiors of display, an effective pairing of means and end.

The Sculpture Objects Functional Art and Design (SOFA) Fair in Chicago is held annually in the fall at the city's Navy Pier. SOFA sponsors an annual student competition for what is known as a Connect Lounge at the SOFA Expo. The connection sought is between the vendors and visitors to the expo, as well as between the students and the larger SOFA community.

In 2015 *Paper + Air* was a winning Connect Lounge collaboration between students from Professor Deborah Schneiderman's graduate thesis studio and Professor Alex Schweder's graduate seminar simply titled *Inflatables*, both in Pratt's Interior Design department. The installation takes advantage of inflatable structures, inherent material and critical qualities.

According to Schneiderman:

> *Paper + Air* is based on the idea of a city as a place of constant change. The project considers the
> life of a city, unifying past, present and future through forms that are found in the overlap between
> expansion and contraction. The elements are readily transportable without compromising spatial
> impact.
>
> (Schneiderman, n.d.)

This lounge utilized two major components. A large lantern-like structure signaled the location of the lounge. The lantern was made using Rhino and Grasshopper; students generated unfolded forms from those digital models, which were used to laser cut each of the lantern's segments, its means of representation and fabrication the same digital file. Each seating element was inflatable, and several times daily the everyday pile of plastic was inflated and deflated in place to create a set of forms abstract enough

Figure 5.9
SOFA, Chicago, 2015 (uninflated). Photo: Deborah Schneiderman

to encourage visitors to experiment with different modalities of occupancy (sitting, lounging, lying down, bouncing).

Kenneth Frampton has suggested that architecture's primary task might be to create an image of its own permanence, *to stand against the fungibility of things and the mortality of the species* (Frampton 1997: 28). Interiors for display propose an active response, charged with the responsibility to a different duration. These interiors mediate the experience of that fungibility, adapting to new research, new acquisitions, new cultural values, or simply new products. The case studies offered here provide examples of aesthetics and material investment purposefully tied to transience that yet address our desire to pursue permanence and novelty in the same place.

Figure 5.10
SOFA, Chicago, 2015 (inflated). Photo: Deborah Schneiderman

NOTES

01 *Oxford English Dictionary* definition.
02 From their website: "BOFFO is a multi-disciplinary not-for-profit arts and culture organization. Since 2009 it has led a critically acclaimed effort to present innovative art, architecture, fashion and design in public or unused space. In doing so BOFFO has presented the work of more than 400 artists and designers, through exhibitions, residencies, large-scale installations, performances and more. BOFFO is the conduit between the emerging and the established, the obscure and the adored. BOFFO is always on the move, repurposing spaces. BOFFO strives to make all projects free to the public. BOFFO believes in art and design as a vehicle of change—a way to improve and enhance the quality of life of our communities and of individuals. BOFFO believes in enabling the greatest creative talent of our time to become powerful forces in shaping social, industry and community landscapes. BOFFO is a 501(c)(3) non-profit, based in New York City."

06 Framing interiority: film sets and the discipline of interior design

Alexa Griffith Winton

The creation of interior spaces for film and the practice of interior design are in many ways closely aligned, with several critical distinctions. Both rely on a broad, multi-disciplinary coordination of elements at a range of scales, including the definition of the spatial envelope, surfaces and textures, colors, objects, lighting, and the control of sound. An interior designer must take into consideration the senses in one's work, including not only how a space looks but also how it feels and how it sounds to the human body, whereas a production designer needs to communicate those things within the mediated space of a film screen. The term *mise-en-scène* refers to the combination of all elements required to create the overall atmosphere of a film. This essay seeks to find overlap between set design and interior design via the examination of aspects of the interior in three recent films.

While a typical interior is designed for permanent inhabitation and use, ephemeral *depictions* of interiors for films must instead create a believable atmosphere of inhabitability, which is communicable to the audience only through visual and aural, not haptic, means. People experience and then map the inhabited interior by the act of moving through it. We use all of our senses to rapidly establish an awareness of place, to orient ourselves, and to apprehend the interior's spatial flows (Hiss, 1991). In this sense a filmic interior is rendered symbolic and must communicate and reinforce critical aspects of plot and narrative without the benefit of touch or smell. This restriction is offset, however, by the ability of a film's director, production designer and cinematographer to precisely shape the viewer's encounter with interior space. Close ups, cropped, and framed views, the manipulation of light and shadow, and the use of interior elements such as colors, surface textures, furniture, objects, and textiles help construct a strong and clear representation of a space, and control any intended symbolic connections and associations between an interior and a character.

This essay explores some of the ways in which the representations of interiors in films make use of both cultural and embodied symbols and references in the depiction of interiors in order to make key points about characters, narratives, and their relationship to key spaces of action and enactment. Using the three films as case studies, this chapter will examine the intersection of light, atmosphere, and character in Cory Fukunaga's 2011 adaptation of *Jane Eyre*; surface, color, and nostalgia in Wes Anderson's 2014 *The Grand Budapest Hotel;* and thresholds, mirrors, and identity in Todd Hayne's 2002 drama *Far from Heaven.*

JANE EYRE (2011)

Since 1910 there have been at least five major film versions of Charlotte Brontë's gothic novel *Jane Eyre*, originally published in 1847. Set largely in the rugged Yorkshire moors, Brontë's text is highly evocative, with detailed descriptions of numerous interiors occupied by the eponymous main character, with each interior reflecting key aspects of Jane's history and experience. In Fukunaga's version of *Jane Eyre* the production design strives for a sense of hyper-naturalism and period authenticity, with meticulously furnished interiors typical of the mid-nineteenth century. It should be noted that descriptions of the events in this story are taken solely from Fukunaga's film adaptation, and that the film diverges from the text in some key details.

Will Hugh-Jones was the film's production designer, and Tina Jones and Greer Whitewick were the set decorators. The film's cinematographer, Adriano Goldman, relied almost entirely on available light—daylight, candles, and lamps—during filming. This not only helps create a believable period atmosphere, but it is of critical importance to the depiction of the film's interiors and subsequent associations between these interiors and the main characters. The use of light—both daylight and that deriving from sources such as candles—is an essential tool in the construction of the film's atmosphere.

The evening scenes in particular feature areas of high contrast between light and dark, with the flickering of candles and firelight creating dark pools of shadow and enhancing this dramatic lighting. Visually this light effect is close to the techniques used in German expressionist films as well as those of the slightly later film noir genre. The dense and layered shadows in the film, and the concomitant uneven and flickering light that dances across the faces of the characters, borrow directly from these earlier forms of film and function as "a device by which the filmmaker communicated a simultaneous, secondary narrative to the viewer" (Franklin, 1980: 178).

The most important interior in the film is Thornfield Hall, where Jane encounters Edward Fairfax Rochester, the mysterious and unpredictable man whose secrets are both embodied and concealed within the rambling, ambiguous spaces of the house. Thornfield is depicted as a magnificent but confusing and gloomy stone manor house, with the perimeters of rooms typically obscured by shadows, eliding boundaries and obscuring thresholds.

Figure 6.1
Jane Eyre. Directed by Cary Fukunaga. Santa Monica, CA: Focus Features and London: BBC Films, 2011

Figure 6.2
Jane Eyre. Directed by Cary Fukunaga. Santa Monica, CA: Focus Features and London: BBC Films, 2011

There is no attempt in the film to provide clear, logical understanding of the plan of the house; rather it is shown as an episodic series of interiors with very limited shots of connecting spaces such as stairs and corridors. This provides a strong sense of spatial ambiguity and suggests that the house, like the man who owns it, is essentially unknowable. This is further enhanced through the dense layers of textiles, furnishings, and objects that imbue the house with an atmosphere of both age and wealth characteristic of the English country house (Girouard, 1978). The furnishings are an eclectic mix of periods and styles, with vernacular country chairs, English Regency dining furniture, and various examples of continental art and decorative objects presumably collected by Rochester on his frequent trips to Europe.

Textiles play a significant role in the interiors of Thornfield, with tapestries and elaborately upholstered furniture displayed throughout the public areas of the house. These textiles contribute both to the sense of Rochester's wealth but also to his secrets. In fact, a tapestry conceals Rochester's most terrible secret, revealed to Jane on the day they were meant to marry. A secret door hidden beneath a Flemish tapestry leads directly up to the garret in which he has concealed and imprisoned his dangerous and mad wife, Jamaican-born Bertha Antoinetta Mason, whom he married for her fortune many years before Jane's arrival at Thornfield.

The viewer gets only a fleeting glimpse of Bertha's barren quarters, which are utterly stripped of furniture and objects of all kinds. The walls are simple plaster and her one window is barred. This scene is filmed in daylight, and Bertha's room is bright and evenly illuminated, in stark contrast to the interiors below, so that the density of textiles, objects, and shadows that defines the main house is completely absent, leaving the characters completely exposed to each other and themselves.

Stanley Kubrick's 1975 film *Barry Lyndon* is an important precedent for Fukunaga's *Jane Eyre*. Kubrick, along with production designer Ken Adam, sought to create a seamless eighteenth-century atmosphere in this film, which is based on William Thackeray's 1844 novel of the same name. Several key interior scenes in *Barry*

Figure 6.3
Jane Eyre. Directed by Cary Fukunaga. Santa Monica, CA: Focus Features and London: BBC Films, 2011

Figure 6.4
Jane Eyre. Directed by Cary Fukunaga. Santa Monica, CA: Focus Features and London: BBC Films, 2011

Lyndon were filmed using only candlelight, although camera technology in 1975 did not allow for the entire film to be shot without electrical lighting. Rather than the brooding, Romantic atmosphere of the lighting in *Jane Eyre*, Kubrick and Adam used candlelight to reinforce the glittering artifice of eighteenth-century aristocratic activities (Robey, 2009).

THE GRAND BUDAPEST HOTEL

In contrast to the gloomy spatial ambiguity of Thornfield Hall, the interiors depicted in Wes Anderson's 2014 film *The Grand Budapest Hotel* provide the viewer with a clear sense of orientation and clarity, as well as of the grand scale of the hotel itself. This desire to clearly map out interior spaces, and to show how the film's characters move through them, is a feature of many of Anderson's films. In the animated film *The Fantastic Mr. Fox*, for example, the network of underground tunnels linking the Fox family to their subterranean animal neighbors is clearly mapped, showing all points of connection. In *The Life Aquatic with Steve Zissou*, the eponymous main character takes viewers on a journey through his ship, The Belafonte, via a full-scale bisected model, providing a highly detailed section view of the vessel's complex sequences of interior spaces.

The Grand Budapest Hotel is a tale of a lost world, as told through the story of the hotel's concierge, M. Gustave H. It was filmed in Germany inside a large, early twentieth-century department store. There are two iterations of the hotel in the film: the grand, sumptuous, pre-Second World War version, and the bleak Soviet-era hotel which, save for a few key features, has had all traces of the original hotel interior obliterated.

The earlier hotel features a large stained glass-covered atrium spanning the lobby. Anderson and production designer Adam Stockhausen provide the audience with many views and scenes emphasizing both the vertical connections between the interior spaces via the grand staircase and a tiny red lacquered elevator, always with the lobby as a central spatial anchor. Additionally there are a number of scenes that provide a sectional perspective of the hotel through the use of long tracking shots of characters moving through its numerous rooms and corridors, emphasizing the sequencing of spaces from private to public (Dunne, 2015).

Figure 6.5
The Life Aquatic with Steve Zissou. Burbank, CA: Touchstone Pictures, 2004

Figure 6.6
The Grand Budapest Hotel. Directed by Wes Anderson, CA: Fox Searchlight Pictures, 2014

The highly detailed representation of Old World European luxury displayed within the original Grand Budapest, derived from a careful study of top pre-Second World War hotels across eastern Europe, is in direct contrast to the views of the exterior. Full-scale views of the hotel and its perpetually wintery landscape are provided through the use of either obviously hand-drawn two-dimensional renderings with no sense of architectural depth or perspective, or a miniature scale model. Cropped shots of the exterior, confined mainly to the vertical section of the entry way and immediate environs, focus on the surface decoration and the purples, pinks and gold with which the pale pink plaster exterior ornament is accentuated.

The original hotel, whose interior suggests a fusion of Beaux Art spatial grandeur and abstract Jugendstil ornament, is contrasted with a subsequent renovation in which the interior is transformed to a dreary space with a drastically lowered illuminated ceiling with harsh fluorescent lights in place of the original warm incandescent lamps and chandeliers. This ceiling obscures the upper registers of the hotel and the original glass ceiling, making it much harder to read the layout of the overall space. Dull browns, acid greens, and yellows replace the original saturated pinks, reds, and purples of the original hotel. The sinuous curves of the Jugendstil-style original are replaced with sharp, angular, gridded surfaces, and nearly all original ornament and detail is gone. In place of this ornament, the walls are studded with a profusion of absurdly literal plaques identifying nearly every element within the interior. The majority of the surfaces in the post-war hotel appear to be industrially manufactured, whereas those of the original hotel—like those of the Secessionist movement—required craft and handwork to achieve. The only potentially gratuitous label in the original hotel is the hat embroidered with the words LOBBY BOY, worn by Zero Mustafa, one of the film's main characters, suggesting that a sense of identity and clarity of orientation in the earlier iteration of the hotel is lost in the post-war version.

The main element of the hotel's lobby, and one of the only details of the original hotel retained in the subsequent renovation, is the grand staircase. Similar to the staircase in Charles Garnier's Paris Opera, completed in 1875, it features two connecting stairways joining both wings of the hotel via the intersecting grand central staircase.

Figure 6.7
The Grand Budapest Hotel. Directed by Wes Anderson, CA: Fox Searchlight Pictures, 2014

Figure 6.8
The Grand Budapest Hotel. Directed by Wes Anderson, CA: Fox Searchlight Pictures, 2014

A grand staircase serves both as a practical connector between the interior levels and as a social space in which to theatrically present one's self by simply ascending or descending its steps. (Bergdoll, 2000) In the pre-war Hotel Budapest, the concierge desk occupies the intersection of both side stairways with the central staircase down to the lobby floor. The concierge's office is warm and efficient, with red lacquered mail slots and Jugendstil desk lamps. Thus, as concierge, M. Gustave H. is embedded within the very heart of the hotel. This central role is emphasized by his meticulous attention to every detail, his memory of all the personal details of his guests, and his deep interest in their well-being.

Figure 6.9
The Grand Budapest Hotel. Directed by Wes Anderson, CA: Fox Searchlight Pictures, 2014

As the story of the original hotel and the charismatic M. Gustave H. unfolds, the contrast between the surfaces and colors in the two versions of the hotel becomes increasingly obvious. The post-war hotel is almost completely devoid of staff as well as guests, in direct contrast to the bustling atmosphere of the pre-war institution.

A square reception desk manned by one seated employee has replaced the circular desk of the original hotel; a plan view of the round desk shows four hotel staffers busily at work. This reception desk also features elaborate carved decorations that clearly reference the designs of the Viennese Secession, particularly those of Joseph Maria Olbrich. In the post-war hotel there is also a bank of vending machines, accentuating the fact that guests are largely on their own. The charmless and mostly empty modern hotel serves to emphasize the loss of the world inhabited by M. Gustave H; its drabness is meant to elicit nostalgia for his long-vanished world.

FAR FROM HEAVEN

Todd Haynes' film *Far from Heaven* is set in Hartford, Connecticut, in 1957. The narrative centers on Cathy and Frank Whitaker, who live with their two children in a large Colonial Revival house, surrounded by a lush and almost unnaturally colorful garden. While outwardly they project an image of idealized married life, their relationship is unfulfilling, for different reasons. Frank is a closeted gay man desperately and unsuccessfully trying to repress his sexuality, while Cathy spends her days attempting to forget her deep loneliness by trying to be a perfect housewife, looking after their two children and managing their family home. She eventually finds solace in her African American gardener, Raymond Deagan, and Frank finds love with another man.

Conformity is a central theme in the film, with its emphasis on the great pressure exerted on both Cathy and Frank to hold fast to the prescribed social conventions of the day. Their house embodies these pressures. It features a perfectly maintained, white clapboard Colonial Revival exterior, while the interior is a strangely incongruous mix of antique and mid-century modernist furniture. Social conventions and the protagonists' accompanying behaviors are contained and policed within the boundaries of this private space. As Jean Baudrillard has suggested, domestic furniture and its arrangement throughout the home reinforce the social structures of a given historical period. The furniture's role is to "personify human relationships, to fill the space they share between them…. They have as little autonomy in this space as the various family members enjoy in society" (Baudrillard, 2005).

In this context the disharmonious interior décor of the Whitaker's home clearly mirrors both the state of their failing marriage and their respective efforts to assemble and define their own identities as distinct from those imposed on them by social convention. The house, stylishly and meticulously maintained by Cathy and her maid Sybil, betrays a struggle for identity: antique furniture rooted in the past, or modernist furniture that has made a clear and conscious break with historicizing form and ornament.

The palette of the film is one of lush, highly saturated colors. Much of the film takes place in autumn, with the New England trees displaying majestic reds, oranges, and yellows. The interiors are very dark, especially in contrast to the brightness of the exterior shots. There is a pronounced blue cast to the evening interior scenes, with the obvious artificiality of this hue highlighting the characters in the act of performing, rather than living, their idealized lives.

The symbolic associations of thresholds, doors, and windows are exploited throughout the film. One of the early scenes features Cathy standing in the threshold of her house watching as her children are picked up by their school bus. Her body and her identity are contained and framed within the boundaries of the house.

In addition to the front door, the Whitaker house features numerous glass doors leading out into the garden, creating a strong visual connection to that natural (if highly manipulated) world outside. Cathy and Raymond's friendship begins in her garden, and subsequently exists entirely in the world outside the domestic

Figure 6.10
Far from Heaven. Directed by Todd Haynes, Santa Monica, CA: Focus Features and Vulcan Productions, Seattle, WA, 2002

Figure 6.11
Far from Heaven. Directed by Todd Haynes, Santa Monica, CA: Focus Features and Vulcan Productions, Seattle, WA, 2002

Figure 6.12
Far from Heaven. Directed by Todd Haynes, Santa Monica, CA: Focus Features and Vulcan Productions, Seattle, WA, 2002

realm. Raymond never enters the Whitaker home and when Cathy visits him at his home she is also not invited over the threshold. Instead they speak outside. Concomitantly, Cathy's ostracization is triggered when a local society reporter, at the Whitaker's to interview Cathy, observes her through the glass doors speaking to Raymond in the garden

The one exception to this division of interior and exterior, public and private, occurs when Cathy brings inside the flowering branches of a tree she and Raymond discussed. She displays them in a vase on a table in the middle of two of the terrace doors looking out on to the garden, bringing a small element of the outside world inside. This small gesture—visible from the garden—signals the degree to which Cathy wants to bring Raymond into her private affairs, transgressing that threshold between public and private. The vase is shown again later in the film, the red petals of the branches' flowers highlighted by the sapphire blue light used to illuminate nearly all of the night-time scenes. The vase is transformed into a melancholic symbol of Cathy's loneliness, compounded by the impossibility of her friendship with Raymond.

In additional to establishing the boundaries between public and private life, interior thresholds and door-ways serve to underscore the emotional distance between Cathy and Frank (Winton, 2013). Edith Wharton, in her highly influential interior design advice book, *The Decoration of Houses*, references the powerful abilities of doors to either welcome or prohibit, writing "while the main purpose of a door is to admit, it's secondary purpose is to exclude" (Wharton, 1897). After Frank has confessed to Cathy that he cannot control his homosexuality and has fallen in love with another man, they have a discussion in the dining room. Frank is in the center of the room while Cathy remains at the room's threshold, standing in the short passageway that connects the kitchen to the dining room rather than stepping into the dining room itself.

Mirrors are used throughout the film to accentuate the elaborate performances Cathy and Frank engage in to maintain their illusion of happily married life. In interior design, mirrors can be used to give the illusion of more space, to reflect light, and to create visual interest. On a symbolic level, however, mirrors suggest duplicity and artifice (Alexander, 1985). Mirrors in *Far from Heaven* perform both functions. For example, the viewer sees Cathy at her dressing table, getting ready for bed, and Frank is only visible as a reflection. Similarly, when Frank first encounters the man for whom he leaves Cathy, the image features Frank, his reflection, and the reflection of his new love as he enters the room, suggesting that Frank is starting to see his true identi-ty—a gay man.

Far from Heaven is a homage to the numerous 1950s films depicting characters who defy the constrictive boundaries of social convention, and there are many direct references to the films of Douglas Sirk. In Sirk's

Figure 6.13
Far from Heaven. Directed by Todd Haynes, Santa Monica, CA: Focus Features and Vulcan Productions, Seattle, WA, 2002

Figure 6.14
Far from Heaven. Directed by Todd Haynes, Santa Monica, CA: Focus Features and Vulcan Productions, Seattle, WA, 2002

1955 social melodrama *All That Heaven Allows*, for example, a wealthy suburban woman falls in love with her much younger gardener, exposing class-based stereotypes, hypocrisy, and social repression. A large picture window is a key feature of the film, and a defining element in the relations between these two key characters. The window serves as a boundary or threshold—or, in the words of Jean Baudrillard, a caesura, dividing the socially unfettered and authentic world of the gardener's natural environs and the civilized yet artificial realm of the upper-middle-class suburban home (Baudrillard, 2005).

In each of the three films discussed, critical elements of interior design—independent of architecture—are used to create and support the narrative, the atmosphere and the depiction of characters. Without verbally describing or explaining, the production design borrows interior design techniques—from light to surfaces and orientation, to thresholds and spatial boundaries—to form an intrinsic part of the atmosphere. These films prioritize the interior and the critical ways in which characters inhabit and respond to it; architecture is depicted only schematically as a way of providing context, and otherwise bears little relationship to the physical and symbolic elements that comprise the films' interiors.

The precision of the spatial and visual narratives constructed within these cinematic interiors—each derived from close readings of historical interiors and their combinations of multiple disciplines at every scale—have likewise influenced the practice of interior design. The framing of the moving human figure, for example, appears in the catwalk-like entrance to the Brasserie Restaurant, designed by Diller+Scofidio in New York City (2000). The long, gently sloping passageway from the outside to the interior of the restaurant operates much like the grand staircase in *The Grand Budapest Hotel*, drawing attention to guests as they enter and depositing them conspicuously in the center of the dining room. Wes Anderson translated his cinematic aesthetic, itself drenched in his knowledge of film history, to the realm of the permanent interior in Bar Luce, the café inside the Fondazione Prada, designed by OMA and completed in 2015. While Anderson described how Italian films such as Luchino Visconti's *Rocco and his Brothers* (1960) and Vittorio de Sicca's *Miracle in Milan* (1951) influenced the design of Bar Luce, he also stressed that the space was intended to be experienced from any angle or perspective, without the framed views provided by the movie camera (Fondazione Prada, n.d.).

The Roman architect and theorist Vitruvius defined the essential qualities of good architecture as *firmitas* (structural integrity and strength), *utilitas* (utility or practical usefulness), and *venustas* (beauty or delight) (Vitruvius, 1999). Through intensive focus on the interior realm, *Jane Eyre*, *The Grand Budapest Hotel*, and *Far from Heaven* reinforce the power of the interior to transcend these and other canonical requirements demanded of architecture, offering new symbolic, spatial, and visual experiences to viewers and inspiration to interior designers.

07 Infrastructural interiors

Deborah Schneiderman

Infrastructural interiors exist either without architecture at all, within a structure that is not typically considered an inhabitable architecture, or where the functionality of the interior is networked. Places of infrastructure—which can be defined as physical places of interconnectivity, a utility that provides the infrastructure for a public service, or as a replicable building model—are critical sites for interior investigation. When one considers infrastructure, the typical association is with physical places of interconnectivity; for example transportation, communication, or utilities. In a more current definition, infrastructure has become understood far beyond this limited scope to include replicable building models that maintain an organization or information network. As individual buildings become reproducible products no longer uniquely designed by architects, but rather engineered for function, they can be defined as infrastructure (Easterling, 2014: 11–12). Likewise, a reproducible interior element set within an architecture can transcend that architecture and become a networked infrastructural interior condition.

There exist several typologies for infrastructural interiors, which can be described by function and by program. This chapter will explore three primary infrastructural typologies: infrastructure as infrastructure, the adaptive reuse of infrastructural interior space for human inhabitation, and the networked interior understood as infrastructure. The three typologies are analyzed through case studies of various programs including subways, parking garages, libraries, and privately owned public spaces (POPS).

INFRASTRUCTURE AS INFRASTRUCTURE

It is critical that the design and materiality of infrastructural spaces are determined in such a way that they meet the requirements to maintain the functionality of that infrastructure. The design strategies might be purely functional, but might also become place-making within a city. In considering infrastructural spaces, what often first comes to mind are those that were not designed for human inhabitation. The stepwells of India, long-forgotten and centuries-old subterranean structures, are being re-evaluated, due to drought, for their ability to collect and store water. Early stepwells were rudimentary subterranean sites for water storage and collection, appearing between the second and fourth centuries A.D. By the eleventh century, stepwells had evolved into complex and ornate excavated infrastructural interior spaces (Lautman, 2013). In a well-recognized contemporary example, the designers at Emery Studio incorporated a form of ornamentation, though theirs is functional, within an infrastructural interior with anamorphic wayfinding graphics for the Eureka car park in Melbourne, Australia, in 2008.

Figure 7.1
Agrasen Ki Baoli stepwell. Photo: Victoria Lautman

Figure 7.2
Eureka car park interior view. © Garry Emery Studio. Photo: Gary Emery

Figure 7.3
Biosphere "lung," interior view. Photo: Deborah Schneiderman

The interiors of infrastructural spaces, however, typically exist without ornamentation. The visually significant interior of the cooling tower at the Monterotondo Marittimo geothermal power station, built in Italy
in 1958 and modernized in 2002, and the "lungs" at Biosphere 2 (1991–1993) in Oracle, Arizona, house
interiors that were designed entirely for technical functionality, yet they have received substantial attention
for their spatial appearance. The "lungs" at Biosphere were designed to prevent the sealed inhabitation
from imploding during its period of occupation. During the day, the heat of the Arizona sun caused the
air inside the facility to expand. So, to avoid the large pressure difference that this created, Biosphere 2's
engineers included expansion chambers termed lungs. Each chamber was a cylindrical tank with a flexible
synthetic rubber membrane that covered and sealed its top. As the air in Biosphere 2 expanded due to
the heat of the day and contracted in the cooler nights the membranes rose and fell (Dempster, 1999: 35).
The columns within the lungs were a significant and extraordinary feature, not for their embellishment but
for their function; they only rested on the ground when the pressure within the biosphere was at its lowest
in order to keep the roof from falling to the floor. As the pressure increased, the columns rose above the
floor surface and remained disconnected from it until the pressure reduced again. The aesthetic of the
interior was purely one of functionality, with the critical materiality being synthetic rubber and water. The

synthetic rubber was specified for programmatic function: expansion and contraction. Water collected from condensation within the Biosphere held in a tank below the membrane. It was stored for uses such as fire suppression, but crucially it maintained the lungs' humidity so that the synthetic rubber membrane did not crack and fail (Biosphere, 2015). The functionality of this interior environment affected all the senses and was unintentionally place-making.

Figure 7.4
This Way. © Linnaea Tillett and Karin Tehve. Photo: Seth Ely

Alternatively, installations can purposefully make place where it was not initially intended within a functioning infrastructure that is typically not inhabitable and is only passed through. *This Way*, a 2008 installation designed by Linnaea Tillett and Karin Tehve, is situated within two Brooklyn Bridge underpasses and arguably makes place in a zone that is an exterior space with an interior condition. Formed from two discrete light systems—linear white fiber optic cable and a grid of blue LED lights—the interiorized zone created by the installation makes place as a beacon that welcomes and leads pedestrians to the bridge (Percent for Art, n.d.). In a more interior condition, abandoned subway stations, which are typically passed through within a moving subway car, have also garnered attention as sites for installations. In the New York City subway system several stations have been shut down as train lengthening and resulting platform extensions made them redundant. In 1956 the platform at Dekalb station was lengthened to accommodate longer trains, forcing the closure of the nearby Myrtle station. In 1980 Bill Brand and Theresa DeSalvio installed Masstransiscope, a station-long installation at Myrtle that utilizes a technique borrowed from the zeotrope, a child's toy. The optical experience generates an animated scene that radically affects the interior experience within a subway car (Brooks, 2010: 6).

The infrastructural site might also be one that is part of an infrastructural network designed for human occupation, such as a subway station. The subway station is of particular interest to the topic of interiors beyond architecture as it is an excavated site and not within a built structure. As it is a transportation system, the design of a subway system is defined as an infrastructural interior. Additionally, the interiors of subway stations are typically designed as parts of a networked system where interior specifications are determined by their requirements for use and then replicated throughout the system. Often the finishes of all the stations on an individual line are systematically linked as wayfinding devices, enabling riders to readily identify which segment of the system each station is associated with. Typical subway stations, those that are simply points along a path, have only limited functional differences as infrastructural interior sites. Differences can include station naming or mapping, with all other fixtures and finishes following format. Atypical stations might be more radically differentiated through a connection to their neighborhood or as a site for public art. The subway station interior is a critical site of infrastructural interior design as both an active station as well as one that has been adaptively reused. The design of a subway station's length is often determined by the length of the trains that travel through it. Also, the materiality is determined by its durability and ability to be cleaned. Some stations become critical nodes or even landmarks in a system.

Overlook: Atlantic Terminal

Allan and Ellen Wexler's Overlook (2007) at New York City's Atlantic Terminal functions simultaneously as a node and as a landmark. According to Lynch, there exist two distinct types of nodes: those that are junctions of paths and those that exist due to a concentration of a single type of use (Lynch, 1960: 47–48). As a node, Overlook is both a point of reference and a critical junction in the path of the city's subway system and the Long Island Railroad. As a landmark, which is typically a physical structure such as a building, sign, or geographic feature used by an individual to better understand and navigate the built environment, it is a readily recognizable built element. Critically, Overlook is particularly compelling as a unique interior landmark that is also inhabitable and can be passed through. In his description of landmarks, Lynch notes that they can be observed but not passed through (Lynch, 1960: 48–49). Overlook is unique as a landmark as it is at once an interior, a threshold that can be passed through and a recognizable urban architectonic

Figure 7.5

Overlook (2009), view from above. © Allan and Ellen Wexler in collaboration with di Domenico + Partners, LIRR Atlantic Terminal. Commissioned by Metropolitan Transportation Authority Arts & Design. Photo: John Bartelstone

Figure 7.6
Overlook (2009), view from below. © Allan and Ellen Wexler in collaboration with di Domenico + Partners, LIRR Atlantic Terminal. Commissioned by Metropolitan Transportation Authority Arts & Design. Photo: Rob Wilson

element. *Overlook* occurs at the threshold of ground level and the underground and is designed to remind observers of the rocky outcroppings at scenic-view rest areas that occur along national highways. It is conceptualized as "a place to observe the theater of people." The artists considered these areas reminiscently as "the places our parents pulled into on long summer car trips. Are we almost there? A much-needed break in the expected and everyday. A place to regroup and to rethink, a retreat. *Overlook*, due to its recognizable form, becomes a landmark and natural meeting point, as a break in a journey, a place to pass through" (Wexler, n.d.).

Overlook celebrates the balance between mathematics and nature. Although the overall form can be understood as a representation of nature, it equally inhabits the built environment as it is constructed from the same tile finish as the station around it, causing the form to be pixelated and clearly man-made. It questions the relationship between nature and mathematics and between the rendered and the pixelated, creating a balance between abstraction and representation. *Overlook* in its construction celebrates the unique interiority of the subway system. It is meant to remind us of the subways' "subterranean existence and speak about excavation, strata and geology" (Wexler, n.d.).

ADAPTIVELY REUSED INFRASTRUCTURAL INTERIORS

As the needs of a city change, evolving technologies and shifting land-use patterns can necessitate systems or buildings changing their use and, sometimes, that the fabric of a place shifts entirely (Brooks, 2010: 2). When land-use patterns shift, some infrastructures become defunct, leaving their structures underutilized or unused and unoccupied. The shells of these now unnecessary systems can be adaptively reused to serve a new or shared purpose through a redesign of their interior. When nodes of a system become underutilized, the possibility for a relevant *time share* or *twist* program, where the originally intended program and a new symbiotic program can alternate or share space to make full use of the underutilized structure, becomes advantageous (Wood and Andraos, 2010: 113–114). A subway station can become defunct as a consequence of an entire system or a large portion of it being shut down or as a more singular elimination of an individual unit.

New York City's High Line, a park on an abandoned above-ground railway which is arguably an exterior environment with an interior condition, has prompted a deluge of adaptive reuse proposals for underground stations and tracks that are no longer used. These include the Lowline in the same city, eleven derelict stations in Paris and the London Underline. Gensler's 2015 proposal for the London Underline continues the functionality of a networked system from the original program for a subway into a newly networked transportation system for pedestrians and cyclists that includes cultural and retail spaces. The Underline plan proposes that all spaces be powered by Pavegen, a kinetic energy system that converts footsteps into electricity. The London scheme would rely on the city's acceptance of alternative transport and would be the first citywide infrastructural interior network of its kind (O'Sullivan, 2015).

The parking garage functions as an adaptively reused infrastructural interior, both as a space that is systematized and regulated by a rule set in its construction and as a node in a transportation system. The parking garage as a design site is rich fodder for prefabricated and/or mobile interior insertions. The floorplan of the typical parking garage is generated with a relatively regular module; it maintains a standard incline and is a space that can be considered interior and exterior at once. Arguably the parking garage is a place of interiority. It comprises a ceiling and a floor, and it provides a space of at least partial enclosure that is protected from the elements (as much as a car requires protection). Though it is technically a building, it is designed for the requirements of a car as its primary inhabitant, and not for human inhabitation. Its architecture is typically

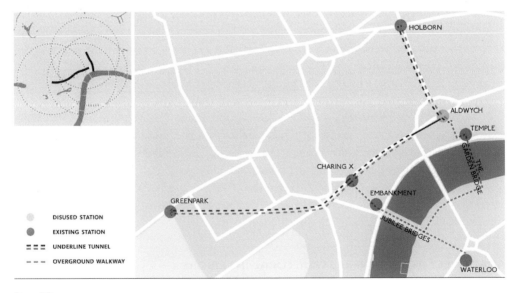

DISUSED STATION
EXISTING STATION
≡≡≡ UNDERLINE TUNNEL
--- OVERGROUND WALKWAY

Figure 7.7
London Underline proposal map. © Gensler

Figure 7.8
London Underline cycle tunnel. © Gensler

Figure 7.9
London Underline pedestrian tunnel. © Gensler

secondary to civil engineering strategies, placing it in a category more aligned with bridges or tunnels rather than architecture (Schneiderman, 2016).

There are at least 105 million parking places in US cities, and a growing number of these—about 50 per cent—are underused (Burns, 2015). The design of a parking garage in North America, as in other parts of the world, is based on the relatively regular module of the car. This spatial rule set affords the potential for a modular adaptive reuse strategy to give a garage a new purpose, either residential or commercial. Considering recent strategies to eliminate personal car ownership through the promotion of better biking conditions, car sharing, and more robust public transport, the need for parking garages is decreasing. Due to this diminishing necessity, the use of a parking garage might be mapped to utilize the space alternately or simultaneously for parking and an additional type of inhabitation.

SCADpad

The SCADpad project employs a twist program strategy and approaches the rehabilitation of the parking garage as an adaptive reuse of the garage to coexist with dorm or living spaces. The dimensions of the modular living units and interstitial community spaces are derived from those of the parking spaces. The interior is at once interior and exterior, making possible the multiple programs that are layered into the site. The placement of the dwelling units and the common areas are determined in a way that best acclimatize those areas for inhabitation and function. The parking garage is a deep-plate construction (as it is designed for cars

Figure 7.10
SCADpad, pod under construction. © Savannah College of Art and Design (SCAD)

and not human inhabitation, the requirement to have light reach the center of the space was critical to its original program). By placing the living pods close to the edges, natural light is brought through.

The strategy for building a parking space-sized living unit is in line with the larger micro-housing movement that exists both within and outside of cities. Within cities, micro housing has been popularized as it allows people to potentially live close to a city center at a more affordable cost while reducing the need for vehicles. There is a spatial and social trade-off to the small dwelling unit; typically such structures include shared community spaces that not only provide relief from the small dwelling size but also an opportunity for residents to meet. Additionally some choose the micro-housing lifestyle as a sustainable strategy that takes up a small footprint and therefore requires fewer utilities for thermal comfort and makes available less space in which to store unnecessary items. The average US parking space is 135 square-feet, so the design for a unit that fits within a single parking spot would cost little to heat or cool (Burns, 2014). The proportions of such habitations and standardized dimensions would also mean they were easily transportable, making it possible for them to become part of a larger networked system.

In addition to the living units, SCADpad incorporates shared community spaces that include a community garden. Fiber optics are employed in the design strategy to bring the light available at the garage's outer edges into interior spaces such as the garden, which has a need for daylight. The project also integrates sustainable strategies: a filtered greywater recycling system that repurposes runoff water from the sinks and showers to irrigate the community garden, a waste-processing system, and provisions for composting. The environment also includes a private patio for each unit sized to one parking space, two lounge areas and an interior park (Burns, 2014).

Figure 7.11
SCADpad, exterior view of North America pod within garage. © Savannah College of Art and Design (SCAD)

A growing interest in sustainable living, which includes reduced car ownership (Rosenthal, 2013), arguably has led to a decrease in demand for parking. The SCADpad project considers a strategy for the reuse or programmatic twisting of a potentially redundant typology.

THE NETWORKED INTERIOR

A set of interiors can comprise a networked infrastructural system. As previously noted, the scope of the definition of infrastructure has come to include replicable building models that maintain an organizational or information network, hence a replicable interior that is part of an information network can also be understood as infrastructure. This hypothesis will be analyzed through brief case studies of two typologies of networked interiors: public libraries and POPS.

Public libraries

A public library is by its programmatic intent a networked information system and is arguably a prototypical infrastructural interior space. The form of the building envelope is not necessarily relevant to the network but its interior components are, in so much as card catalogs bookcases etc. are typical and replicable standardized elements. These interior elements are repeatable structures engineered for function and, as such, library interiors can be considered infrastructural (Easterling, 2014: 11–12). The Brooklyn Public Library system comprises 58 branches and one central library (Brooklyn Public Library, n.d.). The branches comprise networked system of libraries that link neighborhoods through a shared resource. The libraries are important nodes in a network and in the city. They are points of reference within the city as they contain a critical type of use, but could arguably also be considered as a point of destination, though on an information path rather than a path of linear travel.

POPS

The New York City POPS program was developed to incentivize zoning in response to a 1961 zoning resolution in the city (Kayden et al., 2000: 1–2). The program consists of 525 spaces within or adjacent to buildings that were granted additional floor area or related waivers in exchange for providing public interior or exterior space. While the POPS are concentrated in mid-town Manhattan, they also occur at other locations in the city, in three buildings in Brooklyn and one in Queens (The Municipal Arts Society, n.d.)

The addition or maintenance of a POPS requires adherence to a very specific rule set that prescribes design criteria for the inhabitation of the spaces, both interior and exterior. The most essential criteria for the occupation of interior spaces include specifications for seating, planting and trees, lighting and electrical power, litter receptacles, and public space signage. Larger spaces are also required to provide a selection of additional amenities, the number of which is determined by square footage. Options for additional spaces include art, children's play spaces, kiosks, and dining (The City of New York, 2007: 43–49). The POPS, by intent, should encourage free public occupation, which is a unique phenomenon for the interior as its occupation is typically privatized, either as personal or commercialized space. The interior furnishings and fixtures within the POPS are not required to be precisely the same in every space; however, they are arguably part of a replicable system because they are required to follow a prescriptive set of criteria and are hence networked and a part of the urban infrastructure. Though many of the POPS have managed to remain relatively anonymous and underutilized, several, including the David Rubenstein Atrium at 61 West 62nd Street and the Philip

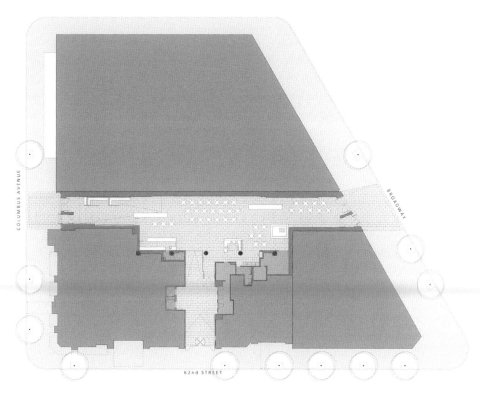

Figure 7.12
David Rubenstein Atrium plan. Courtesy of Tod Wiliams and Billie Tsien Architects I Partners

Figure 7.13
David Rubenstein Atrium. Courtesy of Tod Wiliams and Billie Tsien Architects I Partners. Photo: © Nic Lehoux

Morris Company pedestrian space at 120 Park Avenue, have become critical infrastructural interior nodes in the POPS network. The systemization of POPS elements, which are not necessarily a part of or affixed to the building, are prescribed to make the interior inhabitable and even, as indicated in the code, comfortable, defining the interior space as an autonomous networked set. The spaces have become destinations, and their information is networked solely because they are places of urban interiority.

CONCLUSION

A robust consideration for the design for infrastructural interiors is critical to interior spatial design and sustainable building practice and is clearly situated within the topic "interiors beyond architecture." The design strategies for the interiors of networked subway systems, which typically exist without a building at all, are crucial to human well-being, perception of place and wayfinding. The implementation of twist adaptive reuse for an infrastructural interior, rather than demolition or complete adaptive reuse, allows the initial program to continue with a new symbiotic relationship. Finally, the design for a networked interior can transcend the building envelope, hierarchically elevating the design for repeatable and reproducible interior elements.

THE HYPER-INTERIOR

The texts in this section each address a different extreme at the periphery of the discipline. As aspirations for exploration increase, so do the risks and strains on humans living in extreme environments. Interior design enhances human well-being through the careful creation of spatial components and conditions, particularly important in unfamiliar and extreme environments. Some spatial strategies approach the interior as a continuous ecological system made up of layers of controlled atmospheres and processes, all integrally linked through a shared environment, much like natural landscape. This idea of controlled environmental conditions to produce a particular inhabitation of space suggests a questioning of the very notion that interior design must happen inside.

PROVOCATIONS:

- How can design for extreme interiors inform more "typical" interiors?
- Does the "interior exterior" have a different sensory environment than the "exterior"?
- In the context of historical conceptions of the landscape, how might interior territories propose new relationships between built spaces and ecological systems?

08 Interiors for extreme environments

Gregory Marinic

Interiors beyond the conventional parameters of architecture encompass a broad range of speculative spatial strategies conceived for extreme conditions on Earth and in outer space. Impacted by climate change, the future of life on our planet is being fundamentally rethought to address shifting socio-ecological imperatives. Responding to these challenges, engineering has served as the primary discipline advancing the potential for human occupancy of extreme environments. Since the late twentieth century, however, designers across the disciplines have collectively shaped the development of extreme environments on Earth and those beyond its atmosphere. With this in mind, supporting and sustaining human well-being amidst volatile ecological conditions represents an area of increasing criticality central to the design of interior space.

Emerging in the late 1950s during the Cold War, the global reach of space-oriented culture has transformed our collective expectations for living in space alongside more speculative applications on Earth. Framing a perspective via utopian theory and futurism, this chapter focuses on exemplars of extreme environmental design that emphasize interiority. It examines theoretical projections, cinematic visualizations, fantastical prototypes, and built forms that have promoted greater awareness of living in extreme environments. More specifically, this chapter considers the impact of the Space Age, social shifts, popular culture, film, and technological achievements that have expanded design discourse within the realm of hermetically-enclosed spaces. This research surveys the mid-twentieth century impact of space exploration and futurist influences on the development of spacecraft and autonomous communities. It considers socio-economic, climatic, and dystopian conditions as catalysts for the design of extreme interiorities today.

MIGRATORY UTOPIANISM: TOWARD AN EXTREME INTERIORISM

Utopia offers the critical historian, theorist, or designer a provocative point of engagement—a haunted longing for the potentially better world which exists somewhere between reality and the improbable. In the 1960s, utopian projects became increasingly achievable through spatial experiments on Earth, as well as speculative proposals and built environments conceived for outer space. Utopianism is a theoretical concept that has undergone continual transformation. In 1516, Sir Thomas More—an English lawyer, social philosopher, Renaissance humanist, and Roman Catholic saint—coined the term *utopia* to embody his vision of an ideal and imaginary island (More, 1998: 4). He described a range of alternative political arrangements and social organizations that significantly contrasted with the continual upheaval of medieval European states. In his *Utopia*, communal land ownership, gender equality, and religious tolerance stood in marked contrast to reality. Based on monastic communalism, More traced the conceptual origins of utopia to the Greek words for *no-place* (ou-topos) and *good-place* (eu-topos). Since his time, this ambiguous and autonomous "place" has remained a realm of inquiry for theorists, philosophers, historians, and designers.

By the twentieth century, "utopia" had become thoroughly embedded within the social promise of modernism (Tafuri and La Penta, 1976: 12). It shifted from a conceptual nowhere within the minds of philosophers and transformed into a fantastical somewhere in the ponderings of artists and designers. The celestial

Figure 8.1
Utopia, woodcut image by Ambrosius Holbein (1518)

became terrestrial and the abstractions of philosophy, literature, and art became increasingly worldly. At an urban scale, Kazimir Malevich's utopian towns, Georgii Krutikov's flying cities, Mikhail Okhitovich's patterned collectives and Friedrich Kiesler's space settlements came to illustrate the most avant-garde suprematist projections of this future as an autonomous alternative to normative conditions on Earth. Furthermore, Le Corbusier's urban projects from the 1920s and 1930s reflected the heroic phase of utopian modernism, while his desire for "sun control" and "exact air" proposed a human-controlled future which would modify the most fundamental aspects of ecology (Le Corbusier, 1967).

By the 1960s, the spatial autonomy of closed systems was embodied at scales ranging from metropolitan conurbations to room interiors. The *Dome over Manhattan* (1960) proposal by Buckminster Fuller and Shoji Sadao reimagined New York with a 1.8 mile-high geodesic dome spanning the entire width of midtown Manhattan that sought to regulate weather and reduce pollution. Walking City (1964) by Archigram envisioned building massive, artificially intelligent mobile robotic structures that freely roamed a post-apocalyptic landscape and moved wherever resources or manufacturing were needed. The *Environment Bubble* (1965) project by Reyner Banham and François Dallegret proposed an adaptable structure made simply by means of inflation. Their concept attempted to do away with permanent structures, while lessening the constraints of conventional building practices. It represented an extreme spatial potentiality not otherwise exploited—at once embodying autonomy and ephemerality. In the years that followed, many of these sensational visions of the future came to be viewed as utopian fantasies, yet their dream-like parameters were not entirely insurmountable as autonomous, deployable constructs conceived for extreme environments.

FROM THE SPACE AGE TO CINEMATIC FANTASY AND BUILT REALITY

In the 1950s, diverse visions of futurist living in extreme environments emerged alongside the development of competing space programs in the United States and Soviet Union, as well as on the silver screen. The Soviet launch of the Sputnik satellite in October 1957 and NASA's Apollo project and Moon landing in 1969 focused a global consciousness around hermitic environments required by extreme conditions in space exploration. The great promise of Space Age technological innovations fueled widespread propaganda by the American and Soviet governments linked to political dominance, alongside a desire to leverage new knowledge in an increasingly industrial and overpopulated world. The futurist optimism embodied by science became more visible in mainstream culture, yet stood in marked contrast to conservative social conventions, ecological degradation, international contentiousness, and polarized political systems worldwide.

Many of the communal, social, and space exploration experiments of 1960s utopianism were eventually perceived as naïvely misguided and unsustainable. In 1982, leading Marxist theorist Fredric Jameson reflected on utopianism by proclaiming: "Today the past is dead," and "…as for the future, it is for us either irrelevant or unthinkable." In his book *Archaeologies of the Future: The Desire Called Utopia and Other Science Fictions*, he claims that the utopian impulse is of critical importance to contemporary architecture (Jameson, 2005: 13). Jameson interrogates the collapse of the Soviet system and distinguishes between utopia as a "program" versus utopia as an "impulse." He contrasts the master-planned societies of programmed utopianism with a bottom-up emergence that advances heroic and transformative ideas (Jameson, 2005: 64). His advocacy for utopia similarly invokes the image of the collective, futurist, and revolutionary nature of the avant-garde as the ultimate antidote to top-down autocracies.

Figure 8.2
Space station, *2001: A Space Odyssey*

Space Age and futurist design influences have continually impacted consumer products, fashion, cinematic culture, and interior environments. The worlds of the classic Star Trek television series and Stanley Kubrick's *2001: Space Odyssey* were primarily envisioned as interior spaces in the space stations and domed cities of a future world. Furthermore, earlier philosophical ponderings and cinematic visions slowly came to life in forms intended for space transport and environmental control on Earth. While the limitless potential of early space exploration began to wane, a more pragmatic view of speculative constructs applied to Earth began to rise by the 1990s. The enduring impact of cinematic expression on shaping a generation's presumptions and expectations for extreme environments is undeniable; these creative endeavors presaged the design parameters and aesthetics of actual built work. In an ironic turn, utopian *interior* spaces came to reflect the hierarchical values that Jameson so derided.

Figure 8.3
Le Voyage dans la Lune (A Trip to the Moon) (1902). "Imagining how the space capsule would work...."

SURVEYING EXTREME INTERIORITY

The following case studies survey the twentieth century development of extreme interiors over time and across cultures, describing contemporary extreme environments for space exploration. Space Age ambitions have informed not only the design of spacecraft interiors, but also speculative and built *hermetic* environments on Earth. Otherworldly speculations influenced the dramatic rethinking of a human-controlled future for our planetary atmosphere. These case studies engage the duality of Space Age exploration in parallel with cinematic projections. To illustrate the extent of extreme interiority, three projects were sampled and studied in detail. While seemingly disconnected, these extreme interiors demonstrate how the hermetic needs of space flight imparted similar effects on spatial separation and design aesthetic for interior-focused projects conceived for space colonization. These exemplars—Vostok I, the International Space Station, and Mars 500—include the earliest spacecraft to carry a human and more recent efforts pointed toward the eventual colonization of Mars. They have been paired with similar speculative environments represented in cinematic culture. A reflective conclusion contextualizes these innovations with regard to the current development of suborbital commercial space tourism by Virgin Galactic and Orbital Technologies, as well as their relationship to futurist cinematic visualizations in Kubrick's *2001: A Space Odyssey*.

Vostok I

The space race between the US and Soviet Union began just before the Soviets launched Sputnik I in 1957. Both nations sought to develop human spaceflight alongside increased capabilities in rocket propulsion and jet aviation in competing programs—Project Mercury in the US and Vostok, meaning "East," in the Soviet Union. Vostok I was the first spacecraft to carry a human, Yuri Gagarin, into sub-orbital flight. The launch by the Soviets in 1961 from the Baikonur Cosmodrome in Tyuratam (in what is now Kazakhstan) came 25 days before the first successful sub-orbital NASA flight. To ensure viability prior to the Vostok I mission, test flights of Korabi-Sputnik IV carried a test mannequin named Ivan Ivanovich, a dog named Chernushka, mice and a guinea pig. The Vostok program served as a successful propaganda tool for the USSR; the nation's official commitment to gender equality, for example, was highlighted by the first woman in space, Valentina Tereshkova, who piloted Vostok VI in 1963. Most importantly, after many decades of pondering the seemingly impossible in literary fiction and cinematic fantasy, the Vostok program realized successful human space flight.

Figure 0.4
Vostok I (1961). Spacecraft and original space suit. Photo: NASA

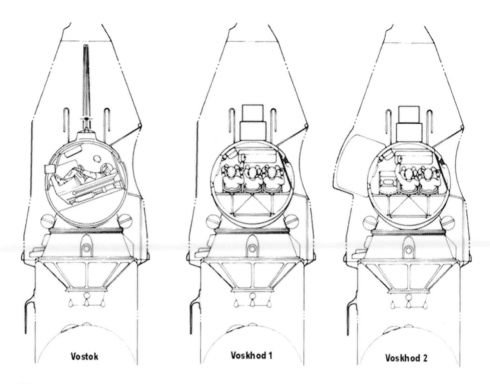

Vostok   **Voskhod 1**   **Voskhod 2**

Figure 8.5
Vostok I (1961). Diagram of cabin interior. Diagram: NASA

Vostok I was designed as a two-module spacecraft composed of a spherical descent module and a service module (LePage, 2011). The descent module was a sphere 2.3 meters in diameter and weighing 2,400 kg (5,300 pounds). This portion of the spacecraft housed the cosmonaut throughout the entire journey. The spherical form was selected primarily due to its naturally high-performance formal qualities. The shape offered a stable, aerodynamic volume that maximized interior space for the passenger and flight control systems. Furthermore, the spherical form offered excellent stability during re-entry. The service module carried all necessary equipment that was not needed for Earth-bound re-entry, including life support consumables, batteries, telemetry systems, altitude control systems, and liquid propellant. The underside of the service module was fitted with radiators that removed heat generated by onboard systems. The interior spaces of the service and descent modules were pressurized to offer a laboratory-like environment that simplified equipment design and thermal control.

By the mid-1960s, the Soviets the Soviets had begun to shift course toward the Soyuz program, the Vostok design continually informed the development of scientific endeavors, military applications, and commercial aviation in the USSR (Ocampo & Klaus, 2013: 78). The Vostok spacecraft was flown more than 800 times, making it the most flown recoverable in history. Space agencies and organizations around the world have benefited greatly from the pioneering efforts of the Vostok program. Since its time, space research has pursued a two-pronged trajectory advanced by space flight innovations and Earth-bound simulations. A variety of methods have been used on Earth to simulate the rigors and challenges of space missions, including inhabitation of caves, oceanic environments, hyper-arid deserts, and hermetic structures.

International Space Station

Initially launched in 1998, the International Space Station (ISS) is a habitable artificial satellite that circles the Earth in low orbit. It is the ninth space station to be inhabited by crews following the US Skylab and Soviet/ Russian Salmut, Almaz, and Mir programs and includes among its components pressurized habitation modules, solar arrays, and external trusses. The ISS offers a research laboratory in which scientists examine in a space-based environment a range of fields including human biology, astronomy, physics, meteorology, and psychology. Most importantly, it allows scientists to test various systems for future missions to the Moon and Mars; it has been continuously occupied by humans since November 2000, representing the longest continuous human presence in space. As an international endeavor, the ISS is supported by five collaborating space agencies: NASA (US), Roscosmos (Russia), JAXA (Japan), ESA (Europe) and CSA (Canada) (NASA, 1999a: 66). It is serviced by various visiting spacecraft, including the American Cygus and Dragon, the Japanese H-II Transfer Vehicle, and the Russian Soyuz and Progress. In 2011, the US Space Shuttle program ended its missions to the ISS, at which time Soyuz rockets became the only transport vehicles to serve the station. Since its inception, the ISS has been visited by cosmonauts, astronauts and space tourists from 17 nations.

The ISS is the first large-scale experiment in space engineering. The initial Russian-built modules were docked robotically, while other modules were delivered by the Space Shuttle and installed by crew members (Coleshill *et al.*, 2009: 870) As a modular structure, the ISS is designed to grow inherently over time in an

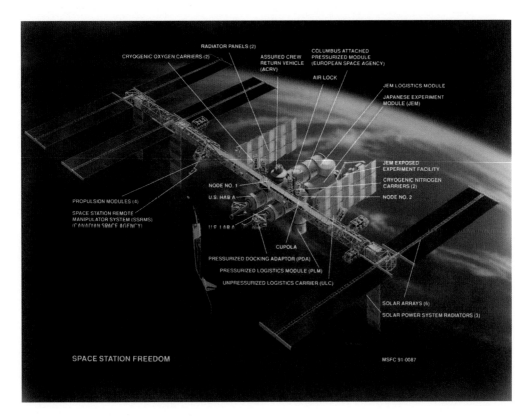

Figure 8.6
Artist's rendering of the International Space Station. Rendering: NASA

incremental and adaptive manner. Like all medium- and long-range spacecraft, it was designed to address two primary needs—navigation and inhabitation. Navigational components include mission operations, general maintenance, suit maintenance, logistics stowage, sub-systems, and laboratories.

The first module, Zarya (Russia), was launched in November 1993 on a Russian Proton rocket. This module provided several primary functions for the ISS, including communications, electrical power, propulsion, and navigational control. Two weeks later, the Unity (US) module was connected to Zarya to provide two pressurized mating adapters. In July 2000, Zvezda (Russia) was launched into orbit and connected to the Zarya-Unity vehicle. Zvezda added habitable chambers including sleeping quarters, a kitchen and toilet room, exercise equipment, data-voice-telecom equipment, CO_2 scrubbers, oxygen generators, and dehumidifiers. The Zvezda module transformed the ISS into a fully inhabitable extreme environment. As a third-generation modular space structure, the ISS is highly adaptable to changes, additions or removals to its existing component-based system. The flexible system is based on pressurized and unpressurized modules. From the standpoint of human habitation, the most important of these modules are Zvezda, Destiny, and Quest (NASA, 1999b: 249). Zvezda enables the ISS to permanently support up to six crew members and living quarters for two.

Housed at the rear of the ISS, Zvezda and its computer system enable the control and navigation of the entire space station; its engines are used to boost the station's orbital capabilities. Within these modules, soft goods made from high-performance textiles replace many conventional constructs due to their space-saving characteristics. For instance, cargo transfer bags are used for containers that hold consumables, hygiene supplies, personal effects, tools, and spare parts, while contingency water containers that house a tank, bladder, and valve assembly are used to move water safely into orbit (European Space Agency, 1993: 30). These innovative products help to lower the weight of the spacecraft and increase the spatial performance of the interior.

The ISS represents a habitable environment designed to counteract adverse effects on the human body, including gravitational forces, atmospheric pressure, and spatial constraints. As such, its design has been carefully crafted not only in the engineering of a robust envelope and state-of-the-art propulsion system but also through humanistic concerns supporting the psychological and physical well-being of crew members (Peacock, Rajulu & Novak, 2001: 130). Although expressing similar motivations with conventional interiors, extreme interiorities demand an exceptionally human-centered and life-dependent approach to interior design contingent upon the most advanced research in engineering, physics, and psychology. Here, the most basic of human functions—breathing, eating, sleeping, and moving—become remarkably complex design problems. Designers of such environments must fully reconsider scenarios that address not only quotidian concerns but also the long-term impact of formal, spatial, and material design conditions. Moreover, designers must anticipate adverse human behaviors that are amplified within the confines of hyper-hermetic spatial configurations. Mitigating the potential for human conflict represented a central aspect of the ISS. Thus, anthropometric considerations became primary drivers at the onset of the design process, whereby the quantitative aspects of human-centered design were mobilized to address the qualitative influences of human behavior. This realm of inquiry—human factors—engages the psychological, physiological, formal, spatial, and material considerations of interiority. For the ISS, human factors research addressed issues ranging from spatial hierarchies related to sleeping, eating, and socializing to the material properties and durability of all surfaces making direct contact with the human body.

The Destiny module was activated in February 2001 as the primary research facility for the US on the ISS. It represents NASA's first permanent, orbital research station since Skylab was deactivated in February 1974. Destiny arrived at the ISS as a preconfigured and entirely prefabricated assembly providing electrical power,

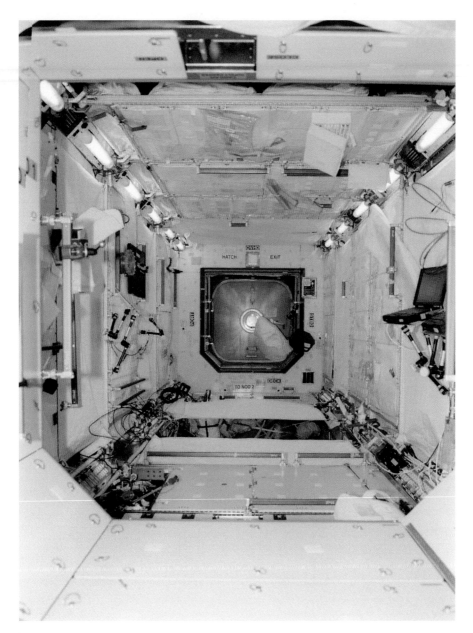

Figure 8.7
ISS Destiny, interior. Photo: NASA

cooling water, air revitalization, temperature regulation, and humidity control. It offers a pressurized facility in which scientists conduct research into fields that include biotechnology, physics, and material sciences. In addition to the primary assembly, two end cones contain hatch openings allowing astronauts to enter and exit the station in pressurized zones. These spaces remain open until the need arises for them to be environmentally isolated. The module is 28 feet long by 14 feet wide, composed of three cylindrical sections,

Figure 8.8
2001: A Space Odyssey, cinematic still image

and offers 3,700 cubic-feet of pressurized space. One of the primary features of Destiny is an optically pure, 20-inch telescope-quality glass window used for observation. Crew members use this large portal to digitally photograph, film, and record the Earth's changing surface and to visually connect with a dramatically framed view of their planetary home. A manually operated shuttle protects the window from micro-meteoroid and orbital debris strikes. The interior of Destiny represents, willfully or not, a real-life manifestation of the fantastical cinematic ponderings of 1960s science fiction embodied by *2001: A Space Odyssey*.

Mars-500

Mars-500 was a collaborative experiment pursued by Russia, China, and the European Space Agency between 2007 and 2011 in preparation for a potential manned flight to Mars. The project attempted to examine human behavior and psycho-social isolation within a purpose-built environment on Earth. The Mars-500 facility included four hermetically sealed and interconnected habitation modules, representing an interplanetary spacecraft, and one external module that served as the "Martian surface." The 72 square-feet habitation module was sized to reflect the spatial dimensions of an actual spacecraft. In July 2010, its "mission" to Mars launched with six male volunteer astronauts housed in a hermetic environment at the Russian Academy of Science's Institute of Biomedical Problems in Moscow. The mission was modeled as a full-length, high-fidelity simulation of a 520-day mission, including the outbound flight to Mars, planetary orbit, landing, surface exploration, return to orbit, and the return journey (Botella *et al.*, 2016: 900). In an effort to frame the nature and sensation of isolation, communications with mission control were artificially delayed. During its mission, the crew performed more than 100 research experiments that examined issues likely to be confronted during interplanetary missions.

Dr Mark Belakovskiy, head of the Mars-500 project, described the crew as the most valuable and vulnerable component of the trip. The nature of deep cocooning, or extreme isolation, is generally viewed as the most significant hurdle of interplanetary travel. Mars-500 research revealed that there are major differences in how individuals cope with isolation over long periods of interior confinement (Tafforin, 2015). Unlike the

NASA space shuttles, whose interior quarters had simpler sleeping arrangements including morgue-like sleep capsules and the use of sleeping bags and hammocks, the Mars-500 interior saw a far more elaborate spatial design. One of the primary differences of the Mars-500 interior is revealed in its materiality wood paneling, as well as built-in provisions including a narrow bed, desk, chair, and shelves for each crew member. Unlike the wildly fantastical visions of spacecraft interiors, these spaces were modeled as ordinary interior spaces on Earth. The familiarity of such spaces was meant to counteract feelings of isolation far from home. Soft goods, made from high-performance textiles, were developed to serve a range of purposes on Mars-500. These included collapsible containers used to hold and secure food, medical supplies, personal hygiene supplies, and tools. High-performance textiles were also employed in the making of acoustic partitions, deployable crew quarters, bedding, and various types of non-flammable crew garments ranging from space suits to onboard clothing.

Apart from individual quarters, the Mars-500 mock spacecraft included collective spaces such as the control room, kitchen-dining room, and living room. Meal preparations involved dehydrated food. The mission was limited to three tons of water, which required crew members to use paper napkins and a steam sauna for personal hygiene. A breath-recycled air system allowed the mock spacecraft to autonomously serve its interior environmental needs.

Although Mars-500 demonstrated that interplanetary missions are indeed possible, astronauts would need to be well vetted to select individuals who could cope well during long voyages. In the Mars-500 simulation, for instance, one crew member became chronically sleep-deprived, one adapted to a 25-hour schedule and one became mildly depressed. It was also determined that the worst psychological impacts would occur early in flight. It is important to note that the day/night cycle of Mars is only 36 minutes longer than Earth's 24-hour cycle (Solcova & Vinokhodova, 2015). While this may not seem significant, the marginally longer days did, in fact, have an impact on crew members in the simulation. As the Mars-based activities represented only 12 full days, researchers believe that the human body would eventually adapt to the longer day/night cycle of the planet. One of the most significant findings of Mars-500 revealed that fluorescent lighting was a significant issue for crew members; the need for natural light was deemed necessary to address long-term depression and sleep disorders.

REFLECTION

With connections to utopian theory and futurist cinema, the trajectory of autonomous interiorities in extreme environments charts a transdisciplinary rise of spatial awareness beyond our planetary constraints. Emerging from origins within our existential consciousness, the history of space exploration has been strongly linked to realizing the speculative closed systems proposed in literature, popular culture, architecture, and the cinematic arts. As constructs that sought to achieve contact with a dream-like world beyond our own, the closed systems surveyed in this chapter represent some of the forms, materials, and supportive systems necessary for sustenance of life on our planet and beyond. Each of these environments was conceived as a closed system—as a self-sustaining environment that functioned autonomously from its surroundings—separated by a discrete and unbreakable boundary. Apart from achieving the near impossible, experiments in space exploration have slowly migrated toward more practical concerns related not only to space exploration, but also to the potential need to sustain life on Earth.

Most recently, the utopian visions of the future embodied in *2001: A Space Odyssey* are incrementally coming to life in built form with the Virgin Galactic space transport vehicles and the Orbital Technologies space hotel. Both projects mobilize early ideas of space tourism and interior experiences that more closely reflect streamlined futurist spaces built on Earth. Kubrick's futurist vision of how an interplanetary Pan American World Airways would take form as a commercial airline navigating outer space has informed the concept for Virgin Galactic. Like the fictional Pan Am proposed by Kubrick, Richard Branson has beguiled the world with a space transport brand linked to a very successful commercial airline on Earth. Familiarity makes the Virgin Galactic project seem intrinsically relatable to our collective expectations for travel, giving credence to the extension of tourism beyond the atmosphere of our own planet. In the stylized branding, articulated interior spaces, high-end service amenities, and established expertise of Virgin Galactic—linked to its earthly sibling Virgin Atlantic—the future seems not only possible, but highly probable. Most importantly, by visualizing space travel that grows organically from our experience with commercial air travel, Virgin Galactic has gleaned a valuable lesson from Kubrick's cinematic ponderings—that familiarity elicits feelings of security, comfort, and home.

Virgin Galactic, in association with the US state of New Mexico and Sierra and Dona Ana counties, has established the first commercial spaceport at Spaceport America. Dedicated in 2011 as the Virgin Galactic Gateway to Space, the 120,000 square-feet terminal designed by Foster + Partners includes astronaut training facilities, the mission control center, visitor lounges, and an exhibition area documenting the history of space exploration and the region. Here, Virgin Galactic takes cues from Pan Am and its iconic Worldport (1960) at John F. Kennedy Airport in New York designed by Turano & Gardner and Walther Prokosh of Tippets-Abbett-McCarthy-Stratton. Both terminals were conceived to serve not only utilitarian purposes, but also to spatially convey innovation in flight. Prototypes for the SpaceShip Two sub-orbital space tourism vehicles are currently being designed by Virgin Galactic. Cabin interiors, seating systems, and high-performance materials are based on design research innovations that were originally conceived for the Virgin Atlantic/ Virgin America product experience. This new spaceship prototype will carry six passengers or the equivalent scientific research payload on sub-orbital flights allowing an out-of-the seat, zero-gravity experience. Adam Wells, head of design for Virgin Galactic, has mobilized his previous experience as designer of cabin interiors, mood lighting systems, airport environments, uniforms, and other service products for Virgin America, Virgin Hotels, and Virgin Cruises—total design experiences based on the shaping of interior performance and atmosphere. Many of these relatively conventional design innovations have provided a foundation for Virgin Galactic spacecraft prototypes, while requiring specific adaptation to "g" orientations and microgravity forces. For instance, the effects of microgravity are mitigated by tethers, ropes, Velcro, and netting that are used to stow items and hold people in place. In spite of such zero-gravity forces, Virgin Galactic has re-envisioned a relatable product experience that reflects the adapted Pan Am conceived for *2001: A Space Odyssey*—a familiar, yet otherworldly interpretation of commercial air travel. In this case, life does indeed imitate art.

In a similar manner, Russia-based Orbital Technologies is developing a space hotel for a commercial space station that will bring Kubrick's Space Station Hilton to life. Clients will be transported to the hotel aboard Russian Soyuz rockets taking roughly 24 hours to reach the space station positioned 217 miles above the Earth. The space hotel will be able to accommodate up to six guests in a luxury environment that will be travelling at 17,500 miles per hour in Earth's low orbit. Here, the Hilton Hotel of Kubrick's dreams is beginning to come to life in built form. Through projects such as Virgin Galactic and the Orbital Technologies space hotel, a transdisciplinary discourse surrounding space travel, climate change, resource depletion, and sustainability continues to develop alongside fantastical experiments in architecture, interior design, the silver screen, and unbuilt work. Collectively, these works are dramatically advancing interest in the study, development, and analysis of extreme environments for human habitation. As these diverse innovations move into the future, they have begun to incrementally realize utopian dreams of navigating and living in extreme environments beyond our planet.

09   Interior landscapes

Brett Snyder

> It is the same in architecture as in all other arts: its principles are founded on simple nature, and nature's process clearly indicates its rules.
>
> (Laugier, 1753)

> In something lying between natural phenomena and built structure there may be new potential for architecture.
>
> (Ishigami, 2010)

Imagine a rendering of a boundless interior, presumably infinite, built of modular systems but unencumbered by the brute rectilinearity of modernist architecture. Curvaceous pedestrian bridges levitate in an infinitely complex dimensional haze. This interior is differentiated, like a forest floor, by random punctuation; modulation of light, crisp scratches, differences in atmosphere. Its surfaces are like skin, created out of microscopic textures. This future was, of course, imagined in a distant past by the architectural speculator Giovanni Battista Piranesi in eighteenth century Italy. The beauty of his drawings lies not just in their spatial complexity and detail but in the way rooms have been hauntingly inflected by natural systems: light, atmosphere, fragmented geometries, and the connection to uncontrollable environments just beyond reach. Interior landscapes, to Piranesi, were the connection between these seemingly infinite interiors and the exterior world just beyond. Interior, depicted here, is a filtered connection to exterior conditions.

While the forms in Piranesi's etchings are not necessarily reminiscent of a typically vegetated "landscape," they are contaminated by the same forces: wind, light, moisture, dust, and dirt (Gissen, 2009) In their complexity one could argue that these images might set some provisional definitions of what a landscape interior might mean to interior architecture. Interior landscape is the conflation of the natural and artificial. It is in the connection of interior to exterior; the past, present, and future woven into one. Interior landscape challenges the conventional interior—its non-porous surfaces, regular ground, and hidden ecologies.

The interior landscape is not simply the conscious integration of materials normally found in landscape, but instead it is applying methodologies typically associated with landscape architecture to the inside. A provisional listing of these methods might include ecological thinking, systems thinking, sustainable practice, passive design methodology, urban design, and even preservation. In this sense the interior landscape can be considered similar to a constructed wetland; a hybrid of natural and synthetic processes. While the general purpose of constructed wetland is to use natural processes to create sustainable environments, one could argue that the interior landscape must have a similar mission at multiple scales. Similarly the interior landscape must connect the user to the environment, taking into account a broad definition of what the environment could be.

Over the centuries many architects, designers, and theorists have grappled with the connections and contradictions that landscape theory offers about interior space. Marc-Antoine Laugier, in his 1753 *Essay on Architecture*, describes the "interior" like pleasures and comforts that natural landscape permits.

> On the banks of a quietly flowing brook he notices a stretch of grass; its fresh greenness is pleasing to his eyes, its tender down invites him; he is drawn there and, stretched out at leisure on this sparkling carpet, he thinks of nothing else but enjoying the gift of nature; he lacks nothing, he does not wish for anything. But soon the scorching heat of the sun forces him to look for shelter. A nearby forest draws him to its cooling shade; he runs to find refuge in its depth, and there he is content.
>
> (Laugier, 1753)

As the traveler continues, he wavers between natural challenges and natural relief, between pain and pleasure. Exterior landscape is the generator of both conditions. And as this traveler seeks to provide refuge that offers only relief he turns to a palette that the landscape provides:

> He wants to make himself a dwelling that protects but does not bury him. Some fallen branches in the forest are the right material for his purpose; he chooses four of the strongest, raises them upright and arranges them in a square; across their top he lays four other branches; on these he hoists from two sides yet another row of branches which, inclining towards each other, meet at their highest point. He then covers this kind of roof with leaves so closely packed that neither sun nor rain can penetrate. Thus, the man is housed…. Such is the course of simple nature; by imitating the natural process, art was born. All the splendors of architecture ever conceived have been modeled on this little rustic hut.
>
> (Laugier, 1753)

Through Laugier's lens, the stronger the connection to natural splendors the more successful the interior.

Theorizing a connection between architecture and landscape was similarly important during the Modern Movement, exemplified through one of Le Corbusier's five points of architecture of 1927: a call for the roof garden. In arguing to replace the traditional pitched roof with an elevated garden, Le Corbusier sought both to create surreal pleasure (by elevating the ground) as well as to achieve urbanistic goals (through the symbiosis of built and natural environments). In *Towards a New Architecture* he states: "Cafes and places for recreation would no longer be that fungus which eats up the pavement of Paris: they would be transferred to the flat roofs" (Le Corbusier, 1931). Here there is a simultaneous call for preservation (of ground) and its novel recombination with architectural form.

Many architects and designers have expressed similar ruminations through their writing and work. Frank Lloyd Wright's Fallingwater (1936–39) pays deference to the river that runs below it. The diagram of the building could be described as a series of floating planes each with a varying connection to the flow of water. These connections are more than strategic views. The planar architecture creates a variety of micro-climates, each with unique wind, sound, light, and moisture levels. Architecture, here, is a liquid affair.

Similarly Casa de Vidro, by Lina bo Bardi, in Morumbi, São Paulo (1949–52), creates a dynamic relationship to the exterior through simple misalignments of its main elements; a shifting ground plane, a hovering courtyard, a floating staircase, and several natural elements including a tree that stitches all of these elements together. The project is at once heroic (as a floating open box) as it is deferential to its environment (with its combination suspended courtyard/skylight) (Instituto Lina Bo Bardi, n.d.).

In these projects there is not an exterior landscape and an interior landscape that are unrelated; instead there is a choreographed connection to the surrounding environment. This project typology stands in contrast to what might typically be thought of as an interior garden. But one must not confuse the term landscape with garden. Interior gardens, such as greenhouses, are typically designed to be separate from an exterior condition. In his book *Manhattan Atmospheres,* David Gissen describes one such project, the Ford Foundation by Roche Dinkeloo and Associates, with Dan Kiley (landscape architect), from 1967. In this vegetated interior "the subtle aromas of plants and flowers and of the newly turned furrow" contrast with the "smells of partially burned hydrocarbons, dioxides and other pollutants" (Gissen, 2014). Here interior and exterior are related only in so far as being in complete contrast and contradiction.

And other projects have radicalized this separation. For example, theoretical works such as Buckminster Fuller's Dome over New York (1960) imagined a sealed atmosphere—a two-mile dome separating an area of mid-town Manhattan, creating a new synthetic natural environment. While the sealed atmosphere in Fuller's dome creates a collective interior, it seems to disregard the world beyond its perimeter. It is simultaneously utopia and an evacuation retreat from a world out of balance.

Perhaps the best example of an interior landscape could barely be described as an interior nor as a landscape at all, but simply as a gradation of atmospheres. Diller + Scofidio's *Blur Building*, an installation for the Swiss Expo in 2002, challenges many notions of what architecture, interior, and environment can be. The project, as stated by Liz Diller, simultaneously highlights the artificiality of a seemingly natural site while heightening one's connection to the actual materials the site is composed of. Diller says:

> The public first catches a glimpse of **Blur** from a distance while walking through the man-made landscape of Expopark. As the visitor nears the lake, the large cloudlike form floating over the water comes into full view. The **Blur** building is… made up of the indigenous material of the site: water. This mist cloud is produced by an artificial fog-making system: lake water is filtered, then shot through an array of nozzles which is regulated by a computer.

> (Diller and Scofidio, 2002)

Blur is simultaneously absence, white noise, media, the absence of media. It is a strategy for making the environment palpable while at the same time inhibiting sight, one of our most basic human functions. Fog is something to avoid, but it is also something that slowly reveals, that makes evident the space between things. In these contradictions the interior landscapes of the future might similarly mask and augment our most basic functions.

Through these examples one can see a range of ways in which architects and designers acknowledge separation and connection between interior and exterior conditions. Each brings up questions of values, especially around individual and collective resources. In the current age, where zero-net-energy architecture is produced to balance out energy demand between the individual and the collective, similar questions abound with landscape. As new typologies for the interior landscape are conceived, might there be similar metrics that consider how the interior landscape contributes to the exterior condition? One current lesson might be borrowed from recent innovations in greywater reuse. Through simple filters greywater can contribute resources from the interior (through passively treated greywater) to the surrounding landscape (as irrigation).

CASE STUDIES

In recent decades interior architecture has grappled with fundamental questions of interior versus exterior condition, with architects, interior architects, and designers employing a range of strategies to achieve an "interior landscape." Projects that could be categorized as interior landscapes include: those that question the notion of ground; projects that include highly complex geometries; projects that use organic material; and projects that have complicated relationships between interior and exterior. But does just having one or more of these qualities allow a project to be classified as an interior landscape?

The interior landscape is not only productive but is based on a close reading of context, which could include issues as far ranging as native plant species to the dominant social activities occurring in a particular place. In this sense the landscape interior considers the ecology of elements within and beyond its boundaries. Similarly the interior landscape raises many questions: the stability and singularity of the ground; the distinction between interior and exterior; and the general desire for materials and atmospheres to be static.

MoistSCAPE

One project that does many of these things while raising an equal array of questions is *MoistSCAPE*, from the Brooklyn-based design firm Freecell. Exhibited at Henry Urbach Gallery in New York in 2004, the project

Figure 9.1
MoistSCAPE installation featuring a hovering blanket of moss over a floor of recycled rubber. Henry Urbach Gallery, New York, New York, 2004. Photo: Ron Amstutz

Figure 9.2
MoistSCAPE installation, lighting and air circulation system. Henry Urbach Gallery, New York, New York, 2004. Photo: Ron Amstutz

was a kind of floating modern interior moss garden. At first glance this project resembles the exuberant angles of deconstructivist architecture; colored planes that self-consciously shift and fold from the ground. On closer inspection one realizes the folds are composed of living moss sitting on perforated metal screens. While the most common interior material found today is sheetrock, the mesh/moss combination is a stark counterpoint. In the architects' words this project was:

> an opportunity to explore the play of the natural within the artificial. We constructed a three-
> dimensional steel matrix inset with panels of living mosses and enclosed within by translucent volume.
> The matrix emerges from the walls and hovers over a groundscape of recycled rubber, which is as
> springy and giving underfoot as the mosses are to the touch of a hand.
>
> (Freecell Architecture, n.d.)

While the conventional interior is composed of non-living and non-porous materials, this interior is composed of porous living materials.

Moreover, there is no hiding of related processes. Fluorescent lights, structure, and the underside of "ground" are all exposed elements. The space is a kind of cubist, surrealist laboratory. The installation lies

Figure 9.3

MoistSCAPE installation, moss carpet detail from above and below. Photo: Freecell Architecture

in suspension, its porous forms subtly leaking from its exoskeleton. Beyond the triangulated planes of moss the installation's breathing apparatus is similarly exposed, its PVC tubes like a giant defibrillator cut into the translucent edging of the installation. The materials and approach are playful, like a folly in a garden. Nothing here is static, from the geometries to the materials, to the exposed atmospheres circulating throughout the gallery.

While this project seemingly inserts the "natural" (moss) into the "artificial" (white box gallery), one could also argue that the project is the "artificial" (geometric slices of moss) inserted into the "natural" (an urban habitat).

What might other manifestations of this project elicit? In other words, what other realizations of the designers' brief (which clearly delineates a landscape interior) might other architects imagine? Might a remix of this project insert a gallery into a forest? Or, perhaps with a little bit of Laugier's logic, use the materials of a forest to produce a gallery? And, seen in the light of synthetic biology, could another manifestation produce an interior that is grown rather than assembled?

Projects like David Benjamin's *Hy-Fi*, which creates bricks from corn stalks, begins to imagine this type of future interior. The project, realized for MoMA PS1, imagines a future in which interiors are grown not built (MoMA PS1, n.d.). The argument is at once sustainable (reducing energy consumption for building construction) as it is aesthetic (with a preference for soft, tactile materials). This future is one in which synthetic biology and architecture are cross-bred to create a Frankenstein architecture cobbled together between living and non-living materials.

Kanagawa Institute of Technology Workshop

A second contemporary project, which could also be classified as a landscape interior, is the Kanagawa Institute of Technology Workshop (KAIT) by the architect Junya Ishigami. While this project does not include complex geometries or methods related to synthetic biology, it is conceived in the logic of landscape with rules that govern the distance between interior structural members. And, like a constructed wetland, it uses minimal material (and the presence of strategic voids) to allow specific kinds of habitation, with little more than air between program rather than walls.

Typically, interior space is conceived as volumes that are needed to allow programs to function. And these volumes are solidified and separated by walls. In the case of KAIT, thin structure is conceived around the space for activities. Where normally walls would fill the space between structural elements, the space is completely open; not only between program areas but also along the entire perimeter, which is sheathed in glass.

Like a forest, the whole is greater than the sum of the parts. In fact the white column structure is only created out of the collective strength of the individual pieces. And also like a forest the space is defined by a single dominant element (the columns), which is then occupied by secondary and tertiary elements (people, desks, plants).

The beauty of this interior, which might be described as quiet exuberance, is manifested through the use of column "slices" of various widths distributed throughout the interior. While the typical column is either square or round in plan, these columns are composed of plate steel arranged in various angles. Any single column would bend but for the sheer force one contributes in the direction where another column is weak. Moreover, the collective pattern that these create might appear random at first but it is organized to create pockets, not unlike what one would find in a forest. Another way to think of this space might be as a series of

Figure 9.4
Kanagawa Institute of Technology Workshop, interior. Architect: Junya Ishigami. Location: Atsugi, Kanagawa, Japan, 2005–2008. Photo: Maurizio Mucciola

Figure 9.5
Kanagawa Institute of Technology Workshop, interior. Architect: Junya Ishigami. Location: Atsugi, Kanagawa, Japan, 2005–2008

vertical fragments that interrupt the horizon. By denying the typical orthogonal grid, Ishigami has used some of the rules of landscape: rules defining the space of an element. And also, similar to a forest, there are no walls; opacity is defined by the proximity of an object in space. Ishigami states:

> [W]hen designing a building I do not simply plan the building by assembling rooms in a spatial composition. Rather, I try to fulfill the planning aspect and simultaneously realize the kind of ambiguity seen within the natural environment as if I were creating a landscape or planning a forest. The uncertainty of ambiguity does not run counter to the element of planning; it too can become a principle for the formation of space.
>
> (Ishigami, 2014)

Another way to think of the logic of this interior is to consider the logic of gardening. When gardeners plant a seed they must take into account the size of a mature plant, not the size of the seed. This anticipates not only growth but also introduces an element of uncertainty. And continuing with this metaphor, plants will grow in a particular direction to gain sunlight. Thus Ishigami positioned columns to allow activities to grow, bleeding into each other's spaces while allowing a collective ecosystem to emerge (Ishigami, 2014).

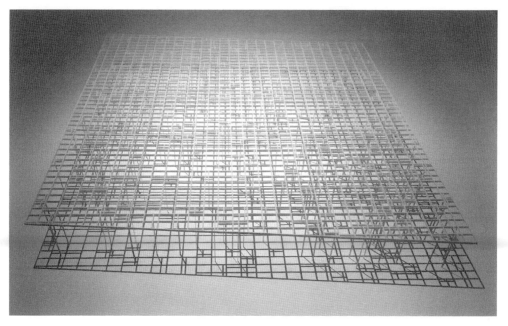

Figure 9.6
Kanagawa Institute of Technology Workshop. Conceptual model featuring an irregular grid of slender plate columns that only resist sheer force because of their collective strength. Architect: Junya Ishigami. Location: Atsugi, Kanagawa, Japan, 2005–2008. Photo: Brett Snyder

The End of Sitting

A third project that could also be considered an interior landscape does not have any organic materials, nor does it have a strong literal connection to the exterior. However, one could argue that this project is incredibly sensitive to the contemporary work environment. Here landscape is an element with agency. The project, *The End of Sitting* by RAAAF (Rietveld Architecture-Art Affordances) and visual artist Barbara Visser, is conceived as a response to the ubiquity of furniture for sitting. While almost all interior spaces are designed for modern furniture, this project takes the opposite approach—denying furniture while only allowing inhabitation. The project is designed with the premise that extended periods of sitting are bad for our health. Yet the modern office interior is never complete without chairs that have been designed to encourage long intervals of sitting. What if, this project asks, our office spaces were designed more like landscape—follies that allowed chance encounters, brief sitting, standing, walking, and leaning. But extended periods of sitting are denied. In fact most furniture will not fit or even be accommodated by this installation's ridges, paths, and valleys.

This project takes on another basic principle of landscape—unstable ground—and uses it to create separation and connections between its inhabitants. The interior installation, which resembles the ghostly landscape paintings of Gerhard Richter, is a series of fluid white forms that meander throughout an interior space. A series of incisions allow a combination of passage and respite. Some of these cuts create paths while others create dead ends. As with the surface of an ocean, its top gently slopes, allowing inhabitants to find a height that fits them. Like *MoistSCAPE* this project is at once natural and artificial.

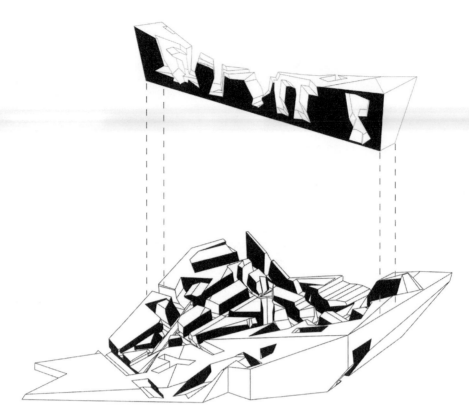

Figure 9.7
The End of Sitting. Client: RAAAF i.c.w. Looiersgracht 60; Art Installation: RAAAF [Rietveld Architecture-Art-Affordances]; Concept: RAAAF | Barbara Visser; Production: Landstra & de Vries supported by Schaart Adventures

Figure 9.8
The End of Sitting. Client: RAAAF i.c.w. Looiersgracht 60; Art Installation: RAAAF [Rietveld Architecture-Art-Affordances]; Concept: RAAAF | Barbara Visser; Production: Landstra & de Vries supported by Schaart Adventures; Photography: Jan Kempenaers

Figure 9.9
The End of Sitting. Client: RAAAF i.c.w. Looiersgracht 60; Art Installation: RAAAF [Rietveld Architecture-Art-Affordances]; Concept: RAAAF | Barbara Visser; Production: Landstra & de Vries supported by Schaart Adventures; Photography: Jan Kempenaers

In the designers' words, "the installation's various affordances solicit visitors to explore different standing positions in an experimental work landscape. *The End of Sitting* marks the beginning of an experimental trial phase, exploring the possibilities of radical change for the working environment" (RAAAF, n.d.).

Equally important, this project thinks of landscape as an intervention into an ongoing process (in this case the almost unconscious act of inhabiting spaces with conventional furniture). By disrupting this process *The End of Sitting* is a kind of radical landscape that asks us to consider that our habits can be rethought through strategic interventions; especially ones that learn from what landscape has to offer (RAAAF, n.d.).

CONCLUSION

Each of these projects challenges the typical interior, whether through geometry, material, or mission. In their gestures they question many of the basic assumptions that have become standard interior practice: rigid geometry, non-porous materials, controlled atmosphere, horizontal ground, and solid walls. While modernism could be considered a relentless march to create contrast between the built and the natural, the interior landscape is part of a counter march: to create meaningful and productive relationships between the interior and exterior of buildings. The landscape interior, like the negative space in the maps of Giambattista Nolli, are strategically fluid connections between interior and exterior. To Nolli the negative space denoted in his maps of Rome connected public exterior to public interior. While the interior landscape may occasionally connect public exterior to public interior, its greater purpose can be thought of as a strategic methodology to consider new possibilities for connection (Tice, n.d.). In some instances this may be by linking materials, in others it might be by reimaging the way water or electricity is understood as a collective resource.

The architectural theorist Reyner Banham has asked what landscape might offer architecture. He has stated: "Underneath lies that basic confusion about the American Landscape—is it wilderness or is it Paradise?" He goes on to say it remains "for serious writers to discover the meaning inherent in the contradiction" (Banham, 1966). And this might give us a place to begin to consider which initial qualities a landscape interior might include, beginning with an acknowledgement of this inherent contradiction.

The counter-march has perhaps best been championed by landscape architects, who by necessity must strategically link ecologies, habitats, and environments. To the landscape architect all elements are in flux. Lawrence Halprin, one such environmental designer who grappled with these issues, theorized the connection in this manner in his landmark book *The RSVP Cycles: Creative Processes in the Human Environment.*

> The essential characteristic of community in the ecological sense is that all of the parts are functioning within their own habitat, that no one element outweighs the other, that each contributes to the whole. Thus the total ecological community has the characteristics of an organism which lives and grows and reproduces itself in an ongoing process.
>
> (Halprin, 1969)

For Halprin, theorizing a methodology to map connections between different realms was a way of mapping invisible connections. In the age of social media and the quantified self we leave more digital trails of our connections. And, more and more, these trails are being concretized in the making of our spaces. The sharing economy itself is one such manifestation, in which objects are in fluid ownership. This area will undoubtedly reshape not just the way we share habitable space but habitable space itself.

What might the interior landscape of the future look like? Matt Damon in the movie *The Martian* may have given us some clue. In using human excrement to produce food on Mars in a duct-taped plastic bubble, the very notion of natural and artificial is moot. This is probably a good clue as to what the future holds.

10   Exterior interiors: the urban living room and beyond

Joanna Merwood-Salisbury & Vanessa Coxhead

Despite the best efforts of high modernist architects and urban designers to privilege openness and continuous space, to do away with enclosure altogether, the contemporary global city is as much an interior condition as an exterior one. Early manifestations of the 'urban interior' appeared in late-nineteenth-century America, when skyscraper architects designed elaborate lobbies mimicking and competing with the streets outside. In the post-war era the invention of new architectural technologies allowed these public-scaled interiors to extend beyond the boundaries of the city block. Air-conditioning, fluorescent lighting, the escalator and long-span structural systems made possible the vast interior spaces characteristic of our contemporary urban landscape: the shopping mall, the office complex and the airport terminal (Koolhaas, 1995, 2000). Intrigued by the possibility of these mega-scale interiors, late-modern architects and designers began to adopt strategies typically associated with urban design in their conceptualization of these spaces (Stickells, 2006; Rice, 2016).[1] At the same time, just as commercial interiors began to acquire the scale and form of the public street, huge swathes of exterior space came under the control of corporate entities or public-private groups such as Business Improvement Districts: organizations that employ almost domestic-scale housekeeping strategies, such as the installation of seating and lighting, in an attempt to render city streets safe and comfortable for middle-class consumers (Mallett, 1994).

Consequently it may be argued that conventional concepts of interiority and exteriority, public and private, are of little use in describing the formal, spatial and social character of the late-modern megalopolis. In this proposition, to suggest a strict division between urban and interior design has become as problematic as drawing a clear line between built form and landscape, between the city and nature. How might we approach the analysis and design of such a confusing territory when conventional design concepts, practices and tools are no longer sufficient? In considering this question, the recent formulation of 'urban interiors' shows much promise. Discussing her self-identification as an 'urban interiorist', the designer and educator Suzie Attiwill has written: 'I am interested in the conjunction of "urban and interior" in relation to the design of interiors and what a practice of interior design has to contribute to the contemporary city' (Attiwill, 2011: 13). Here the discipline of interior design is removed from its traditional, supplementary relationship to architecture, allowing interior design expertise to be applied in broader contexts. The possibility of opening up a speculative space between disciplines, of creating hybrid practices, has been fruitfully explored elsewhere: for example, the positioning of 'landscape urbanism' as a credible form of practice and area of study (Corner, 1999; Waldheim, 2006). While it is not possible to erase disciplinary boundaries altogether, they may be suspended in order to allow different types of knowledge and different ways of working to emerge. Inspired by the discourse of urban interiors, this essay explores the ways in which concepts of interiority have structured the design of urban space from the mid-1960s until today. Beginning with two seemingly oppositional models – the urban living room and the urban surface – it introduces a series of contemporary examples in which concepts of interiority continue to contribute to the creative and innovative design of urban space. Illustrating an urban interiorist approach to the design of city parks, squares, streets and left-over spaces, they rely on strategies of appropriation (involving site-specific reactivation and reprogramming) and scalar confrontation.

THE URBAN LIVING ROOM

Emerging out of post-war critiques of modernist urbanism, the metaphor of the urban living room is based on two seemingly contradictory ideas: the desire to both recapture the spatial character and social potential of the densely populated pre-modern city square (which has a grandeur and scale associated with hierarchical public rituals and ceremonies) and to lend urban space something of the domestic (to make it personal, intimate and comfortable). This rhetorical inversion, in which the exteriors became imagined in interior terms, appeared in the 1960s in reaction to high modernist city planning. For Le Corbusier, Mies van der Rohe and Ludwig Hilberseimer the dominant model of urban space was a continuous ground, a flat plane extending in all directions and forming an endless uninterrupted field on which pristine object-buildings stood. To cover these vast distances, high-speed automotive travel was privileged above pedestrian walkways. Applied wholesale to large areas of new or rebuilt development in the post-war years, this strategy was critiqued for its alienating effect. In an effort to solve this problem, writers and practitioners sought potential solutions in historical models. The critic Jane Jacobs famously praised the narrow nineteenth-century streets of Greenwich Village in New York City as a positive alternative to the wind-swept plazas dividing tower blocks in new housing developments (Jacobs, 1961). Architect and historian Colin Rowe went back even further in time to renaissance and baroque city planning. In his book *Collage City*, Rowe used the courtyard of the sixteenth century Uffizi Palace in Florence as an example of what he called an inverted figure-ground plan, an outside space surrounded by walls on all sides and inhabited as a sort of public interior (Rowe, 1978). For both Jacobs and Rowe these historical urban interiors promoted a civilized sociability and were vital to the performance of citizenship. Influenced by these writers, architects and urban designers began to experiment with inward-looking urban spaces designed to foster human interaction.

The work of sociologist William H. Whyte proved hugely influential in popularizing the urban living room idea.[2] During the 1960s he analyzed a number of the so-called pocket parks in New York City (Whyte, 1980). Using time-lapse photography he studied patterns of movement and occupation in order to extrapolate the principles of successful small-park design. His primary critique of his subjects was that many were designed primarily for visual appeal, or as elements within a larger urban composition, with little thought as to how people would inhabit them. For Whyte, effective pocket parks – like walled gardens, their ancient predecessors – embodied key qualities of interiority: they had plenty of seating and pronounced edges. These edges might not be walls – they could be plants, screens or changes in level – but they offered a similar feeling of containment and security, providing the occupants with a sense of belonging while at the same time preserving their visual connection to the surrounding city. Paley Park, in mid-town Manhattan, is often cited as the archetypal example of Whyte's design principles. Designed by landscape architects Zion and Breen in 1967, this miniature park is surrounded on three sides by high-rise buildings. One enters by ascending a flight of steps. At the top a grid of honey locust trees shades a cobblestoned plaza on which simple metal chairs encourage passers-by to pause and sit. The rear of the space is a high waterfall, with two ivy-covered slabs on either side. The sound of falling water muffles traffic noise, providing an aural boundary between the park and the street. Whyte particularly emphasized the importance of moveable seating to the social function,

Figure 10.1
Paley Park, Zion & Breen Architects, New York City, 1967. ART on FILE

allowing people to alter the environment to their liking, to literally 'make room' for themselves, increasing their sense of control and belonging.

In the late-twentieth-century the belief in the profoundly social function of urban space spread beyond corporate plazas to encompass much larger areas of the city, not just dedicated parks. Beginning in Europe, the urban designer Jah Gehl led a movement to reclaim city streets for pedestrians (Gehl, 2004). While Gehl usually works in collaboration with city authorities, others have taken a more bottom-up approach to the creation of new versions of the urban living room. The work of Rebar, a San Francisco art and design collective, typifies an approach often referred to as 'tactical urbanism'. Sometimes described as 'hacking the city', tactical urbanism uses temporary, low-cost and scalable design elements to activate underutilized outdoor spaces for community use (Lydon and Garcia, 2015: 73). Central to the success of the movement is that it can be implemented quickly, with the temporality of interior design rather than urban design. Like squatters taking over an abandoned building, in 2005 members of Rebar installed some artificial turf, a bench and a tree in a downtown parking space, feeding the meter to guarantee access to the spot. They called the result a 'parklet'. The project led to a larger movement in which parking spaces were transformed into temporary, car-sized parks, usable by the hour, all over San Francisco and in other cities. In 2010 Rebar expanded this idea, creating *Walket*, a modular system of slatted wooden benches, leaners, planters and bike racks designed to reclaim the parking lane for pedestrian use. With domestic scale mix-and-match pieces that can be quickly and easily combined and recombined, the system extends the sidewalk, providing places to sit, relax and socialize.

While these projects provide the means to activate streetscapes quickly and inexpensively, without the need for large-scale capital investment, the same general approach has been successfully adopted by civic entities in several cities. Beginning in 2008 the New York City Department of Transportation closed two of

Figure 10.2
Walklet, Rebar, San Francisco, ongoing; first installed May 2010 © Rebar

Figure 10.3
Walklet, Rebar, San Francisco, ongoing; first installed May 2010 © Rebar

Broadway's four lanes between Herald Square and Times Square and installed a series of *ad hoc* pedestrian plazas made from green gravel glued to the road surface, furnished with plastic planters and lawn chairs (Sadik-Khan, 2015). The project attempted to solve the conflict between huge crowds and fast-moving cars by reducing traffic and offering tired tourists a place to sit. Set up for a trial period, the temporary plazas

Figure 10.4
Visualization of Times Square Reconstruction, Snøhetta, New York City, 2016. © Snøhetta and MIR

served as full-scale tests whose effects could be measured and modified. Snøhetta is now realizing the Times Square portion of the project in permanent form, replacing the lawn chairs with elegant granite benches. Complementing the glowing LED facades of surrounding buildings, the two-toned custom-paved ground surface is embedded with nickel-sized steel discs, activating the horizontal plane by capturing and scattering reflected light. A visual fold in the continuous ground surface, the benches provide pedestrians an opportunity to stop and admire their spectacular surroundings.

THE URBAN SURFACE

The Snøhetta project points towards a more recent model of urban place-making in which concepts of interiority are at play. This is the idea of the 'urban surface', which first appeared in the 1990s in reaction to what was seen as the overly prescriptive agenda of the urban living room. In one sense it may be seen as a revival of the modernist urban plane, with similar aims. But, as Alex Wall has suggested, the emphasis here is not on fixed functional-zones, as in early twentieth century city planning, but on multiple functions coexisting on a single surface and the promotion of dynamic flows of activity across it (Wall, 1999). The motivation behind this approach is to increase social capacity. Rather than dictating use, open and extensive urban platforms are created on which unexpected events might occur. Geographers Don Mitchell and Lynne Staeheli phrase it this way: 'The ideal form for public space is one that allows for a range of activities and for the appearance of a range of identities, but the way that this is managed is left open or unresolved' (Mitchell and Staeheli, 2007: 120). The creation of the late-modern version of the urban surface is aided by new technologies; in particular, computer software that allows designers to create non-Euclidean forms and complex curves. Exploiting the form-making ability of this software, projects featuring ground surfaces that fold into walls, which in turn become seating and ceilings, have become almost a cliché.

At first it might seem that the urban surface model is intrinsically anti-interior, certainly to the concepts of enclosure and privacy with which it is so often associated. However, more recent versions begin to borrow from the interior design tradition. The surface in question has a thickness: it folds and warps, providing corners and pockets for intimate inhabitation. The success of the model depends on the coexistence of multiple scales and types of activity. The surface must allow for roads and buildings, but also for the human body, the private encounter, in order for its full potential to be realized. For example, Avi Laiser and Dana Hirsch Laiser's

Figure 10.5
The REAL estate, AL/Arch, Bat Yam, Israel, 2012. © Avi Laiser

Figure 10.6
Knitted Wonder Space II, Toshiko Horiuchi MacAdam with Interplay Design & Manufacturing, Inc. (net design & construction) and Takaharu & Yui Tezuka, Tezuka Architects (project design), Hakone Open Air Museum, Hakone, Japan, 2009. © Masaki Koizumi

'the REAL estate', in Bat Yam, Israel (2008), features a continuous concrete 'blanket' wall in which biomorphic wooden niches are cut out, forming small private spaces within the surface of the larger public landscape.

The reintroduction of the scale of the body brings us back to arguments supporting the urban living room, but at the same time it opens up another possibility: the application to exterior contexts of pliable, soft materials traditionally associated with interior spaces, such as curtains, wallpaper and carpets, which may incorporate vivid colour, texture and decorative effects. Referencing traditional feminine crafts, the artist Toshiko Horiuchi MacAdam's colourful knitted play structures explore the potential of textiles to become dynamic and three-dimensional, extending their scale and scope beyond the tactile to the tectonic.

Stadtlounge (2005), a plaza in St. Gallen, Switzerland, designed by Carlos Martinez Architekten in collaboration with artist Pipilotti Rist, is an evocative expression of a similar idea. The designers reactivate a previously underused space into a sort of 'city lounge', as the name implies, by literally rolling out the red carpet. The application of a continuous surface of red granulated rubber across pedestrian, recreation and rest areas brings cohesion to an area of irregular and unconnected voids, slowing down movement and tempting pedestrians to stop and touch their surroundings. The thickness, texture and pattern of the rubber is emphasized by the three-dimensional forms that emerge from under the surface: tables, benches, planters, a water fountain, even cars, are swathed in firehouse red. In this way the city fabric (made literal) is softer and more welcoming. Exploiting the semiotic associations of carpet, in contrast with typical plaza surfaces of asphalt or stone, the soft texture provides comfort. It has the capacity to receive impressions, for the wear and tear of habitual use to be made evident on its surface; the marks of human inhabitation are not seen as undesirable, but celebrated.

Figure 10.7
Stadtlounge, Carlos Martinez Architekten and Pipilotti Rist, St Gallen, Switzerland, 2005. © Marc Wetli and Hannes Thalmann

Figure 10.8
Stadtlounge, Carlos Martinez Architekten and Pipilotti Rist, St Gallen, Switzerland, 2005. © Marc Wetli and Hannes Thalmann

APPROPRIATION

The projects described so far concentrate on the provision of comfortable, human-scaled environments within often-inhospitable cityscapes. With their focus on seating and shading devices they present a homogenous, safe and predictable vision of urban public space. In order to reveal a wider range of design propositions, any discussion of contemporary urban interiors must also feature work with a more pointed intent, what Rochus Hinkel has described as 'speculative installations and interactions in the public sphere' (Hinkel 2011:81). This approach shares similarities with the practice of tactical urbanism described earlier. But rather than restricting itself to typical 'urban living room' functions – sitting, eating, socializing in small groups – other forms of interior activity are brought outside and, in the process, transformed by being made public and accessible. This is not an open-ended concept of urban functionality where anything is possible. Instead it is a highly prescribed and specific use of public space, often intended to preserve what scholars and community activists call 'social sustainability', which refers to 'maintaining and enhancing the diverse histories, values and relationships of contemporary populations' (Low, Taplin and Scheld, 2005: 5). When realized successfully, such projects position urban interiorism as a collective and site-specific form of social space production.

Dance-O-Mat is a coin-operated dance floor first installed at various sites in Christchurch, New Zealand, in 2012. Following two damaging earthquakes, hundreds of buildings were demolished and many city blocks reduced to rubble-strewn empty lots, creating a devastating impact on civic morale. In response the ironically named collective Gap Filler produced a moveable outdoor dance floor and sound system made up of a series of banal interior fixtures: a washing machine, a disco ball and plastic flags. Set against the backdrop of a radically broken city, the well-used project produced moments of humour, playfulness and joy. The creators and guardians of the Dance-O-Mat discuss the importance of community acceptance to the success of the project. Such interventions require more than the placement of objects in space; they also require a well-tuned and empathetic understanding of what is needed in a particular place at a particular time.

Figure 10.9
Dance-O-Mat, Gap Filler, Christchurch, NZ, ongoing; first installed 2012. © Fairfax Media NZ/The Press

In a similar way, the work of the English art-architecture collective Assemble focuses on the ability of design to effect social transformation. Questioning normative modes of design practice and shifting towards a hands-on, collaborative working method, the collective is concerned with the way in which even simple, temporary constructions can act as catalysts for community building. For example, The Cineroleum (2010) on London's busy Clerkenwell Road transforms the forecourt of a derelict petrol station into a pop-up cinema. The cinema is formed by the unity of three disparate elements: the concrete and steel structure of the exist-ing petrol station, a bank of tiered seats and an extravagant curtain of silvery drapery. This billowing reflective curtain softens the concrete structure, offering both shelter and a sense of theatricality to the otherwise

Figure 10.10
The Cineroleum, Assemble, London, 2010. © Morley Von Sternberg

Figure 10.11
The Cineroleum, Assemble, London, 2010. © Morley Von Sternberg

banal site. Here the rich and ornate elements of cinema architecture are recreated in industrial, reclaimed or donated materials such as scaffolding and roofing membrane, with careful attention to handmade details. The project is a celebration of the shared escapism of cinema-going: when the curtain falls, viewers are transported far from the grimy site outside into a fantastic interior world.

SCALAR CONFRONTATION

Describing the condition of late-modern architecture and urban design, the architect Rem Koolhaas identified something he called, or the 'Problem of the Large' (Koolhaas, 1995). The space of the city, he said, has become so impossibly vast and complex that traditional design tools and strategies are no longer sufficient to organize it or give it meaning. An unexpectedly simple interiorist approach to this dilemma is to hold firm to the power of the small, the quiet and the private within this metropolitan morass. The final category of urban interior to be discussed here is best termed 'scalar confrontation'. Bringing the scale, form and materials of furniture or domestic rooms into direct confrontation with the urban realm, with little or no threshold or transition, these projects emphasize continual and sometimes uncomfortable exchanges across the public and private divide, turning the sociability of one-to-one interaction into a political gesture. Transportability is often a feature, so as to activate different spaces at different times. This is sometimes expressed via mechanistic forms, with the elements of construction revealed. Hinkel calls such projects 'micro-architectures… small-scale interventions, which are minor in their spatial appearance, less dominant than large-scale buildings or infrastructures. These micro-architectures would not greatly change the aesthetic of a space, but would expand its potential use and allow for appropriations' (Hinkel 2011: 95).

The emphasis on amplifying social exchange is central to the work of Yoshiharu Tsukamoto and Momoyo Kaijima, partners in Tokyo-based Atelier Bow-Wow. Aaron Betsky has described their work as 'rearranging the ordinary' (Betsky, 2006: 97). For example, *White Limousine Yatai* (2003), which takes the traditional Japanese 'yatai', or street-side food cart, and stretches it from its typical 1.5 metre length to 10 metres, following the model of the stretch limousine. In doing so the small-scale charm of the traditional cart is extended to the scale of a banquet, encouraging the strangers seated together to interact over a meal..

Figure 10.12
White Limousine Yatai, Atelier Bow-Wow, Echigo Tsumaari Art Triennale, Niigata, Japan, 2003. © Atelier Bow-Wow

The architect Colin Fournier and the artist Marysia Lewandowska's *Open Cinema* is another powerful example of this approach. Produced for the first time in 2012 as a temporary installation in Guimarães, Portugal, it has been re-presented in Lisbon (2013) and in Hong Kong (2016). The project is a free public cinema, made small and intimate within a large civic location, bringing strangers together at the scale of the domestic television. Though varied in its detail, each edition is based on the same basic design principle: spectators wanting to go in are required to manoeuvre their bodies, bending down underneath the curved exterior structure, entering via one of 16 downward-pointing nozzles into circular holes in the installation's underbelly. Once inside, the spectator's torso is immersed in a cinematic black box, a cool, dark and acoustically sealed cocoon lined with soft materials (cork or upholstery).

While most viewers choose to leave their feet planted firmly on the ground, the temptation to climb inside, to sit or lie within the structure, is apparent. In contrast to the usual cinema-going experience – where the transition between outside and inside, the real world and the filmic environment, is drawn out through a series of intermediary thresholds – visitors to the *Open Cinema* exist simultaneously inside and outside, in both real and virtual space. Their lower bodies revealed, made public, the inhabitants are at the same time anonymous because their faces are invisible.

Taken together, these projects challenge our understanding of public space in the contemporary city and the possibilities for its design. To be public has traditionally meant to be expansive and exposed, open and transparent, to allow for the kind of massed crowds associated with pre-modern squares and marketplaces. As the literature on urbanism reveals, these kinds of spaces were at one time vital to the formation of public opinion, to the expression of political ideas and to the performance of citizenship. But in the twenty-first century, as digital media have become our primary form of communication, public space is no longer covalent with the public sphere. At the same time the existence of a singular 'public' has also been called into question. Scholars have identified the existence of so-called counter publics (groups often alienated from mainstream

Figure 10.13
Open Cinema I, Colin Fournier and Marysia Lewandowska, Guimarães, Portugal, 2012. © Colin Fournier and Marysia Lewandowska

Figure 10.14
Open Cinema II, Colin Fournier and Marysia Lewandowska, Guimarães, Portugal, 2013. © Colin Fournier and Marysia Lewandowska

Figure 10.15
Open Cinema III, Colin Fournier and Marysia Lewandowska, Hong Kong, 2016. © Colin Fournier and Marysia Lewandowska

forms of representation) and alternative public spheres, self-created places in which a variety of identities are expressed and acknowledged (Crawford, 1995). The economic forces and architectural mechanisms that created the modern megalopolis, a place in which concepts of inside and outside begin to lose their meaning, also provide an opportunity for designers to engage with these multiple publics, to understand urban space in new ways, and to make unprecedented interventions. As the projects shown here illustrate, the deployment of interior concepts of temporality, scale, form and materials greatly enlarges what is possible within the urban realm.

NOTES

01   Charles Rice and Lee Stickells have both discussed the adoption of the metaphor of urbanism in the design of large-scale interior spaces, beginning with the work of American architect John Portman in the 1960s, through to the present day.

02   Whyte went on to found the Project for Public Spaces, which continues to research and publish on this topic. See, for example, Project for Public Spaces Inc. (1984) *Managing Downtown Public Spaces,* Chicago: Planners Press/ American Planning Association.

Acknowledgements

This project has been inspired by our many dedicated and enthusiastic colleagues pushing to build critical discourse for interior design. We have been especially inspired by our contributing authors and thank them profusely for their time and dedication, and to the designers who inspired the project in the first place.

Many thanks to Fran Ford at Routledge for her interest in and support for this project. Thanks to Jennifer Divina for reviewing parts of the manuscript. We would also like to thank our colleagues at California College of the Arts and the Pratt Institute for their support and, especially, Anita Cooney, Dean of the School of Design at the Pratt Institute, for her continued support for design research and this project in particular.

Amy Campos
With eternal love and gratitude to Brian, our children Olivia and Casper, and to Mum, Dad and Brad for their endless support and encouragement.

Deborah Schneiderman
My profound thanks to my husband Scott and our twins Chloe and Eli Lizama.

Contributors

Graeme Brooker is Head of Interior Design and Professor at The Royal College of Art, London. He has published numerous books on the interior and, in particular, the reuse of existing buildings.

Amy Campos is Associate Professor of Interior Design at California College of the Arts. Her work focuses on durability and design with special interest in the impermanent, migratory potentials of the interior. The work spans a variety of scales and platforms, from inhabited urban and architectural spaces to object and furniture design. Her essays include "Territory and Inhabitation" (*Interior Architecture Theory Reader,* 2017) "Interior Migrations" (*iijournal*, 2013) and "Optimistic Projections on the Cultures of Mass Consumption and Waste" (*Forward*, 2011).

Vanessa Coxhead is an architectural graduate at Jasmax, Auckland and a recent graduate of the School of Architecture, Victoria University of Wellington, New Zealand. Her current research focuses on urban densification and ideas of neighborliness.

Alexa Griffth Winton is an Assistant Professor of Design History at Ryerson School of Interior Design in Toronto. Her work engages the visual and material culture of the last century, with a focus on the history and theory of interiors. Her research also addresses craft in the industrial and computer ages, and the role of technology in modern domestic design.

Gregory Marinic PhD is Director of Graduate Studies and Associate Professor in the University of Kentucky College of Design School of Interiors. A widely published design scholar and researcher, his most recent publications include Journal of Architectural Education, AD Journal, Design Issues, International Journal of Architectural Research, Journal of Interior Design, and IntAR Journal of Interventions and Adaptive Reuse..

Joanna Merwood-Salisbury is Professor of Architecture at Victoria University of Wellington, New Zealand. Her current research focuses on the history of urban interiors in the United States. She is author of *Chicago 1890: The Skyscraper and the Modern City* (University of Chicago Press, 2009) and a co-editor of *After Taste: Interior Design in the Expanded Field* (Princeton Architectural Press, 2012).

Deborah Schneiderman is Professor of Interior Design in the School of Art and Design at Pratt Institute as well as a registered architect and the principal and founder of deSc: architecture/design/research. Her scholarship and practice explore the emerging fabricated interior environment and its materiality. A widely published design scholar, her publications include authorship of *Inside Prefab: The Ready-Made Interior* (Princeton Architectural Press, 2012) and *The Prefab Bathroom: An Architectural History* (McFarland, 2014). She was co-editor of *Textile, Technology and Design: From Interior Space to Outer Space* (Bloomsbury, 2016).

Alex Schweder works with what he calls "Performance Architecture" through exhibitions that explore the relationships between subjectivity and space. His work has been internationally exhibited and collected, including by the Museum of Modern Art. Schweder's PhD from the University of Cambridge is based on his research into this topic.

Brett Snyder is a principal of Cheng+Snyder, an experimental architecture studio based in Oakland, California, and an Associate Professor of Design at the University of California, Davis. Snyder's research and built work explore the intersection of architecture and media.

Karin Tehve founded KT3Dllc in 2001 to pursue projects in architecture, interiors and site-specific art. She is an Associate Professor of Interior Design at Pratt Institute. Awards include the Building Brooklyn Award and the Lumen Regional Award for *This Way* with Linnaea Tillett, a light installation under the Brooklyn Bridge.

Lois Weinthal is Chair of the School of Interior Design and Professor at Ryerson University. Her research and practice investigate the relationship between architecture, interiors, clothing, and objects, resulting in works that take on an experimental nature. She is editor of *Toward a New Interior: An Anthology of Interior Design Theory* (Princeton Architectural Press, 2011).

Bibliography

"About Brooklyn Public Library," Brooklyn Public Library (n.d.). Online. Available at www.bklynlibrary.org/about [accessed May 22, 2016].

Alexander, R.L. (1985) "The Mirror, Tool of the Artist," *Source Notes on Art* Vol. 4, No. 2: 55–58.

Attiwill, S. (2011) "Urban and Interior: techniques for an urban interiorist," in R. Hinkel (ed.) *Urban Interior. Informal Explorations, Interventions and Occupations,* Germany: Spurbuchverlag: 11–24.

Aubert, M., Brumm, A., Ramli, M., Sutikna, T., Saptomo, E.W., Hakim, B., Morwood, M.J., van den Bergh, G.D., Kinsley, L., Dosseto, A. (2014) "Pleistocene cave art from Sulawesi, Indonesia." *Nature.* Vol. 514, Oct. 9, 2014: 223–227.

Auge, M. (1995) *Non-Places: Introduction to an Anthropology of Supermodernity,* London and New York: Verso Books.

Ban, S. (2014) Voluntary Architects Network, *Lotus 155—Geography in Motion.*

Banham, R. (1966) *A Critic Writes: Essays by Reyner Banham,* Berkeley: University of California Press.

Baudrillard, J. (2005) *System of Objects,* London: Verso Press.

Bergdoll, B. (2000) *European Architecture 1750–1890,* Oxford and New York: Oxford University Press.

Bergdoll, B. and Christensen, P. (2008) *Home Delivery: The Making of the Modern House,* New York: The Museum of Modern Art.

Betsky, A. (2006) "Make it New: Aaron Betsky on Atelier Bow-Wow," *Artforum* 44:10: 97.

"Bianca." Online. Available at ateliermanferdini.com (n.p.) [accessed April 22, 2016].

"Biosphere" (2015) *Biosphere Tour* [Tour].

Birringer, J. (2003) "Marina Abramović on the Ledge," in *A Journal of Performance and Art,* Vol. 25, No. 2, Cambridge, MA: The MIT Press on behalf of Performing Arts Journal, Inc.

Botella, C., Baños, R. M., Etchemendy, E., García-Palacios, A. & Alcañiz, M. (2016) "Psychological countermeasures in manned space missions: 'EARTH system for the Mars-500 project," *Computers in Human Behavior, 55:* 898–908.

Bourriaud, N. (2010) *Postproduction. Culture As Screenplay: How Art Reprograms the World,* Berlin: Lukas & Sternberg.

Braniffinternational.com (n.p.) [accessed March 5, 2016].

Braniffpages.com (n.p.) [accessed February 17, 2016].

Bremner, C. and Rogers, P. (2013) "Design Without Discipline," *Design Issues 29:* 4–13.

Brooker, G. (2015) "Interior Architecture: The Unfixed and the Becoming." Online. Available at www.innermagazine.org/interior-architecture-the-unfixed-and-the-becoming [accessed November 10, 2015].

Brooks, G. (2010) "Reusing and Repurposing New York City's Infrastructure: Case Studies of Reused Transportation Infrastructure," (working paper), New York: New York University.

Broome, B. (2010) "Ace in The Hole," *Architectural Record* 198(4): 56–61.

Buckminster Fuller, R. (1969) *Operation Manual for Spaceship Earth,* Zurich: Lars Muller: 67.

Burns, R. (2014) "Multistorey car park in US transformed into designer micro-apartments," *The Guardian.* Online. Available at www.theguardian.com/cities/2014/jul/09/multistorey-car-park-us-designer-micro-apartments-affordable-housing [accessed November 15, 2015].

Buscher, M. and Cruikshank, L. (2009) "Designing Cultures: Post Disciplinary Practices," Eighth European Academy of Design Conference. The Robert Gordon University, Aberdeen, Scotland. Online. Available at www.researchgate.net/publication/259576511_Designing_Cultures_Post-Disciplinary_Practices [accessed November 15, 2015].

Camper Together, available at camper.com (n.p.) 2016 [accessed January 17, 2016].

"Cappadocia." *National Geographic* (n.d.) Online. Available at http://travel.nationalgeographic.com/travel/world-heritage/cappadocia/#/cappadocia-whirling-dervishes_92983_600x450.jpg [accessed May 7, 2016].

Coleshill, E., Oshinowo, L., Rembala, R., Bina, B., Rey, D. & Sindelar, S. (2009) "Dextre: Improving maintenance operations on the international space station," *Acta Astronautica,* 64(9–10): 869–874.

Corner, J. (ed.) (1999) *Recovering Landscape: Essays in Contemporary Landscape Theory,* New York: Princeton Architectural Press.

Cotter, H. (2004) "Sampling Brooklyn, Keeper of Eclectic Flames," in *The New York Times.* Online. Available at www.nytimes.com/2004/01/23/arts/art-review-sampling-brooklyn-keeper-of-eclectic-flames.html?_r=0 [accessed April 20, 2016].

Crawford, M. (1995) "Contesting the Public Realm: Struggles over public space in Los Angeles," *Journal of Architectural Education* 49: 1, 4–9.

"Cricket," available at taxaoutdoors.com (n.p.) [accessed April 15, 2016].

Davies, B. (2016) "Design for Extreme Environments Project [DEEP]: A Case Study of Innovations in Mediating Adverse Conditions on the Human Body," in Schneiderman, D. and Griffith Winton, A. (eds.) *Textile Technology and Design: From Interior Space to Outer Space.* London and New York: Bloomsbury.

Dempster, W.F. (1999) Biosphere 2 engineering design. *Ecological Engineering* 13: 31–42.

Diller, L and Scofidio, R. (2002) *Blur.* New York: Harry N. Abrams.

Di Raimo, A. (2014) *Francois Roche: Heretical Machinism and Living Architecture of New-Territories.com,* Rome: Edistampa.

Dunne, C. (2015) "How Designers Built the World of *The Grand Budapest Hotel* by Hand," *Fast Co.* Online. Available from fastcodesign.com [accessed February 15, 2015].

Easterling, K. (2014) *Extrastatecraft,* London: Verso.

Edensor, T. (2005) *Industrial Ruins: Space Aesthetics and Materiality,* London: Berg.

European Space Agency (1999) "International space station overview," *Air & Space Europe,* 1(4): 28–33.

Evans, R. (1997) "The developed surface: an enquiry into the brief life of an eighteenth-century drawing technique," in R. Evans (ed.) *Translations from Drawing to Building and Other Essays,* London: Architectural Association: 195–231.

Finney, G. (2016) Interview with Amy Campos, conducted on August 15, 2016.

Fondazione Prada, Bar Luce. Online. Available from: www.fondazioneprada.org/barluce/ [accessed June 15, 2015].

Frampton, K. "Intimations of Durability," *Harvard Design Magazine: Durability and Ephemerality,* No. 3, Fall 1997.

Franklin, J. (1980) "Metamorphosis of a metaphor: The shadow in early German cinema," *New German Critique Vol.* 53, No. 2: 176–188.

Freecell Architecture (n.d.) "Moistscape project description." Online. Available at www.frcll.com/moistscape/ [accessed July 1, 2016].

Friedman, A.T. (2009) "Ship shapes: ocean liners, modern architecture and the resort hotels of Miami Beach," *Designing the Modern Interior: From the Victorians to Today,* Berg NY: Sparke, Massey, Keeble & Martin.

García-Abril, A. (2010) *Ensamble Studio.* Online. Available at www.ensamble.info [accessed July 1, 2016].

Gehl, J. and Gemzøe, L. (2004) *Public Spaces, Public Life,* Copenhagen: Danish Architectural Press.

Gilliam, T. (dir) 1985, *Brazil,* film, 20th Century Fox/Universal Pictures.

Girouard, M. (1978) *Life in the English Country House,* New Haven and London: Yale University Press.

Girst, T. (2003) (Ab) "Using Marcel Duchamp: the Concept of the Readymade in Post-War and Contemporary American Art," *Tout-Fait—The Marcel Duchamp Studies* 2(5). Online. Available at www.toutfait.com/issues/volume2/issue_5/articles/girst2/girst1.html [accessed November 30, 2015].

Gissen D. (2009) *Subnature: Architecture's Other Environments,* New York: Princeton Architectural Press.

Gissen, D. (2014) *Manhattan Atmospheres,* London: University of Minnesota Press.

Gordon, A. (2008) "Adam Kalkin: Divergent Multiplicity," in Will McLean (ed.) *Quik Build. Adam Kalkin's ABC of Container Architecture,* London: McLean.

Gunn, Simon. 1999. "The middle class, modernity and the provincial city: Manchester c.1840–80".

Gender, Civic Culture and Consumerism: Middle-Class Identity in Britain, 1800–1940. Manchester University Press, Manchester.

Halprin, L. (1969) *The RSVP Cycles: Creative Processes in the Human Environment,* New York: Doubleday.

Hensel, M. and Turko, T. (2015) *Grounds and Envelopes: Reshaping Architecture and the Built Environment,* Abingdon: Routledge.

Hildebrandt, H. (2004) "The Gaps Between Interior Design and Architecture." Online. Available at www.di.net/articles/the-gaps-between-interior-design-and-architecture [accessed November 29, 2015].

Hill, J. (2003) *The Actions of Architecture,* London and New York: Routledge. Hill citing W. Benjamin's *The Work of Art:* 22.

Hinkel, R. "Private Encounters and Public Occupations: A methodology for the exploration of public space," in R. Hinkel (ed.) *Urban Interior. Informal Explorations, Interventions and Occupations,* Germany: Spurbuchverlag: 79–87.

Hiss, T. (1991) *The Experience of Place,* New York: Random House.

Huysmans, J. and Baldick, R. (1959) *Against Nature,* Penguin Books.

Instituto Lina Bo Bardi. (n.d.) "Casa De Vidro." Online. Available at http://institutobardi.com.br/?page_id=113 [accessed July 1, 2016].

Ishigami, J. (2013) *Another Scale of Architecture,* Kyoto: Toyota Museum of Art.

Ishigami, J. (2014) *How Small? How Vast? How Architecture Grows,* Germany: Hatje Cantz.

Jacobs, J. (1961) *The Death and Life of Great American Cities,* New York: Random House.

Jameson, F. (2005) *Archaeologies of the Future: The Desire Called Utopia and Other Science Fictions,* New York: Verso Books.

Kayden, J. (2000) New York City Department of City Planning and the Municipal Arts Society, *Privately Owned Public Spaces in New York City,* New York: Wiley.

Kirkham, P. and Weber, S. (2013) *History of Design: Decorative Arts and Material Culture,* New Haven: Yale University Press.

Kleinman, K. and Adams, C. (2012) Interview with Constance Adams: "We Are In This Together," in Kleinman, K., Merwood-Salisbury, J. and Weinthal, L. (eds.) *After Taste: Expanded Practice in Interior Design,* New York: Princeton Architectural Press.

Kleinman, K., Merwood-Salisbury, J. and Weinthal, L. (eds.) (2012) *After Taste: Expanded Practice in Interior Design,* New York: Princeton Architectural Press.

Koolhaas, R. (1995) "Bigness or the Problem of Large," *S, M, L, XL,* New York: Monacelli Press.

Koolhaas, R. (2000) "Shopping," in *Mutations: Harvard Project on the City,* Barcelona: ACTAR.

Kruft, H. (1994) *A History of Architectural Theory: From Vitruvius to the Present,* New York: Princeton Architectural Press.

Lasc, A., Patricia Lara-Betancourt, P. and Petty, M. (2017) *Architectures of Display: Department Stores and Modern Retail,* London: Routledge.

Laugier, M. (1753) *An Essay on Architecture,* trans. W. and A. Herrmann (1977). Los Angeles: Hennessey and Ingalls.

Lautman, V. (2013) "India's Forgotten Stepwells," *Arch Daily.* Online. Available at www.archdaily.com/395363/india-s-forgotten-stepwells/ [accessed December 10, 2015].

Leach, W. (1993) *Land of Desire: Merchants, Power and the Rise of a New American Culture,* New York: Pantheon Books.

Lebel, R. (1959) *Marcel Duchamp,* New York: Paragraphic Books: 77–78.

Le Corbusier (1931) *Towards a New Architecture,* trans. F. Etchells, New York: Dover Publications.

Le Corbusier (1967) *The Radiant City: Elements of a Doctrine of Urbanism to be Used as the Basis of Our Machine-Made Civilization,* London: Faber & Faber.

LePage, A. (2011) "Vostok: An aerospace classic," *The Space Review,* April 2011.

Low, S., Taplin, D. and Scheld, S. (2005) "The cultural life of large urban spaces," in *Rethinking Urban Parks: Public Space and Cultural Diversity,* Austin TX: University of Texas Press.

Lynch, K. (1960) *The Image of the City,* Cambridge, MA: MIT Press.

Lydon, M. and Garcia, A. (2105) *Tactical Urbanism: Short Term Action for Long Term Change,* Washington D.C.: Island Press.

McLuhan, M. and Terrence Gordon, W. (1999) *Understanding Media: The Extensions of Man.* Critical ed. Cambridge, MA. MIT Press.

Mallett, W. J. (1994) "Managing the post-industrial city: business improvement districts in the United States," *Royal Geographical Society* 26(3): 276–287.

Martin, C. (2016) *Shipping Container: Object Lessons,* London: Bloomsbury.

"Massclusivity: Trend Bulletin from Trendwatching.com." Online. Available at trendwatching.com (n.p.), 2016 [accessed 15 January 15, 2016].

Meridian line, Royal Observatory Greenwich. Online. Available at www.rmg.co.uk/royal-observatory/meridian-line-and-historic-observatory [accessed September 29, 2016].

Mitchell, D. and Staeheli, L. (2007) *The People's Property? Power, Politics, and the Public,* London: Routledge.

MoMA PS1 (n.d.) "Hy-Fi by the Living." Online. Available at http://momaps1.org/yap/view/17 [accessed July 5, 2016].

More, T. (1998) *Utopia* (10th ed.), New York: Dover Publications.

Mueller, T. (2014) "Il Duomo," *National Geographic,* February 2014.

NASA (1999a) "Assembly schedule of the international space station: status at June 1999," *Air & Space Europe,* 1(4): 66.

NASA (1999b) "From cold war to international space station: IAF's Amsterdam congress marks 42 years of the space age," *IEE Review*, 45(6): 248–249.

National Park Service Centennial, available at nps.gov (n.p.) [accessed February 10, 2016].

New London Bus, available at heatherwick.com (n.p.) [accessed May 15, 2016].

Ocampo, R. P. & Klaus, D. M. (2013) "A review of spacecraft safety: from Vostok to the international space station," *New Space*, 1(2): 73–80.

Ortega Y Gasset, J. and Bell, A. (1990) "Meditations on the Frame," *Perspecta* 26: 185–90.

O'Sullivan, F. (2015) "Bike paths in abandoned tube tunnels: is the London Underline serious?" *The Guardian*. Online. Available at www.theguardian.com/cities/2015/feb/05/bike-paths-abandoned-tube-tunnels-london-underline [accessed December 5, 2015].

"Overlook for the Atlantic Terminal," Allan Wexler Studio (n.d.). Online. Available at www.allanwexlerstudio.com/projects/overlook-atlantic-terminal-2009 [accessed March 3, 2016].

Pallister, J. (2015) *Sacred Spaces*, 1st ed. London: Phaidon.

Peacock, B., Rajulu, S. & Novak, J. (2001) "Human factors and the international space station," *Proceedings of the Human Factors and Ergonomics Society Annual Meeting*, 45(2): 125–139.

"Percent for Art," The City of New York (n.d.). Online. Available at www.nyc.gov/html/dcla/html/panyc/tilletttehve.shtml [accessed December 1, 2015].

Perec, G. & Sturrock, J. (2008) *Species of Spaces and Other Pieces*, (rev. edn.) Penguin Books.

Pimlott, M. (2007) *Without and Within*, Rotterdam: Episode Publishers.

Pine, B. and Gilmore, J. (1998) "Welcome to the Experience Economy," *Harvard Business Review*, July-August.

Prada 24 Hour Pop-Up Museum. (2012) Available from designboom.com (n.p.) [accessed February 10, 2016].

Privately owned public plazas text amendment adopted by City Planning Commission 09/19/2007 adopted by City Council 10/17/2007. The City of New York. Available at file:///C:/Users/My%20PC/Dropbox/interior-without-arch-projects/pops-code.pdf [accessed May 20, 2016].

"Privately owned public spaces in New York City." The Municipal Arts Society of New York City (n.d.). Online. Available at http://apops.mas.org [accessed May 20, 2016].

RAAAF [Rietveld Architecture Art Affordances] (n.d.) "The End of Sitting." Online. Available at www.raaaf.nl/en/projects/927_the_end_of_sitting [accessed July 8, 2016].

Rice, C. (2016) *Interior Urbanism: Architecture, John Portman and Downtown America*, London: Bloomsbury.

Robey, T. (2009) "*Barry Lyndon*: Kubrick's Neglected Masterpiece," *The Independent*, February 5.

Rosenthal, E. (2013) "The End of Car Culture," *The New York Times*. Online. Available at www.nytimes.com/2013/06/30/sunday-review/the-end-of-car-culture.html [accessed June 14, 2016].

Rowe, C. and Koetter, F. (1978) *Collage City*, Cambridge MA: MIT Press.

Rudofsky, B. (1964) *Architecture Without Architects*, New York: The Museum of Modern Art.

Sadik-Khan, J. (2012) "Making cities work," in *Beyond Zuccotti Park: Freedom of Assembly and the Occupation of Public Space*, New York: New Village Press: 283–296.

Scaglia, G. and Prager, F. (1970) *Brunelleschi: Studies of His Technology and Inventions*, 2004 MIT Press (ed.), Mineola, New York: Dover Publications.

Schneiderman, D. (2016) "On the Fringe," *ii journal*, Vol. 5.

Schneiderman, D. (2016) "Bespoke: Tailoring the Mass-produced Prefabricated Interior," in Schneiderman, D. and Griffith Winton, A. (eds.) (2016) *Textile Technology and Design: From Interior Space to Outer Space*. London and New York: Bloomsbury.

Schneiderman, D. (n.d.) Projects (Description of Paper + Air). Online. Available at www.deborahschneiderman.com/picture-gallery.php [accessed April 10, 2016].

Simmel, G. "Fashion," *The American Journal of Sociology*, Vol. 62, No. 6 (May 1957).

Slade, G. (2006) *Made to Break: Technology and Obsolescence in America*, Cambridge, MA: Harvard University Press.

Solcova, I. & Vinokhodova, A. (2015) "Locus of control, stress resistance and personal growth of participants in the Mars-500 experiment," *Human Physiology*, 41(7): 761–766.

Sparke, P. (2008) *The Modern Interior*, London: Reaktion Books.

Stickells, L. (2011) "Swiss cheese and beanbags: Producing interior urbanism" in Lois Weinthal (ed.) *Toward a New Interior*, New York: Princeton Architectural Press: 180–198.

Tafforin, C. (2015) "Comparison of spatiotemporal adaptive indicators in isolated and confined teams during the Concordia stay, Tara drift, and Mars-500 experiment," *Journal of Human Performance in Extreme Environments*, 12(1).

Tafuri, M. & La Penta, B. (1976) *Architecture and Utopia: Design and Capitalist Development* (4th ed.), Cambridge, MA: MIT Press.

Tice, J. (n.d.) "The Nolli map and urban theory." University of Oregon. Online. Available at http://nolli.uoregon.edu/urbanTheory.html [accessed July 6, 2016].

The Pullman Company, available at pullman-museum.org (n.p.) [accessed April 13, 2016].

The Routemaster Bus (1992) BBC documentary, Perpetual Motion.

Twyford, E. (2016) "Design for Confinement: The Art and Science of Sensory Deprivation Space," in Schneiderman D. and Winton A. (eds) *Textile Technology and Design: From Interior Space to Outer Space,* London and New York: Bloomsbury.

Vitruvius (1999) *Ten Books on Architecture*, trans. I. Rowland, Cambridge and New York: Cambridge University Press.

Waldheim, C. (2006) "Landscape as urbanism," in Charles Waldheim (ed.) *The Landscape Urbanism Reader*, New York: Princeton Architectural Press: 35–54.

Wall, A. (1999) "Programming the urban surface," in James Corner (ed.) *Recovering Landscape: Essays in Contemporary Landscape Theory*, New York: Princeton Architectural Press: 233–250.

Wharton, E. (2007) *The Decoration of Houses*, New York: Rizzoli Publishers.

Whyte, W. (1980) *The Social Life of Small Urban Spaces*, Washington D.C.: Conservation Foundation.

Winton, A. (2013) "Inhabited Space: Critical Theories and the Domestic Interior," in Weinthal, L. and Brooker, G. (eds) *The Handbook of Interior Architecture and Design,* London and New York: Bloomsbury Press.

Wood, D. and Andraos, A. (2010) "Work: Program primer," *Praxis* 8: 111–121.

Young, L. (2000) "Think Tank." The New York Times. Online. Available at http://www.nytimes.com/library/magazine/specials/20001008mag-young13.html [accessed July 1, 2016].

Zeiger, M. (2011) *Micro Green: Tiny Houses in Nature,* New York: Rizzoli.

Index

Note: italics refer to images; 'n' refers to chapter notes.